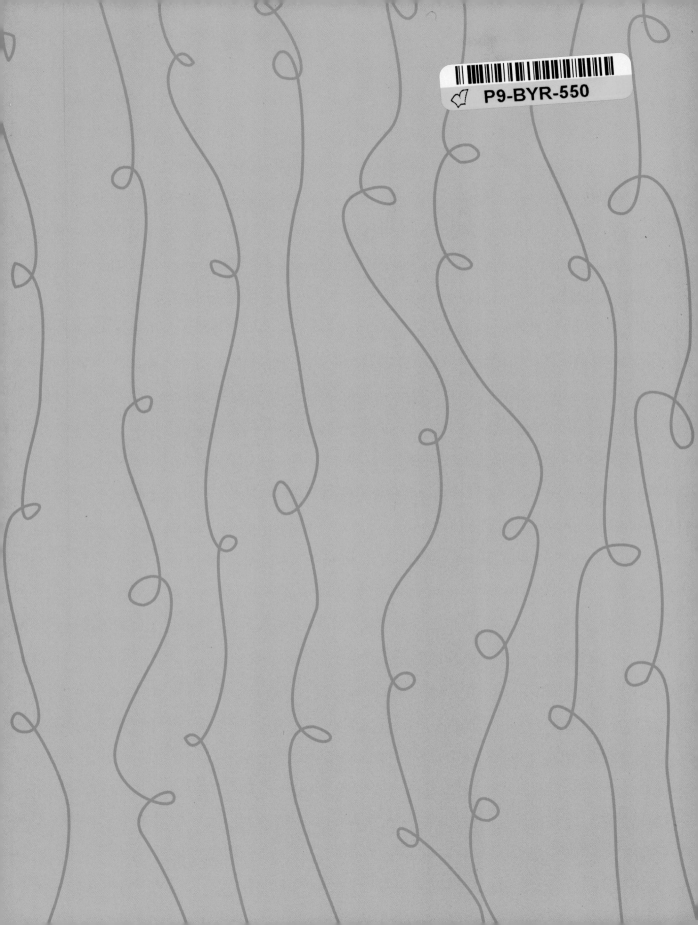

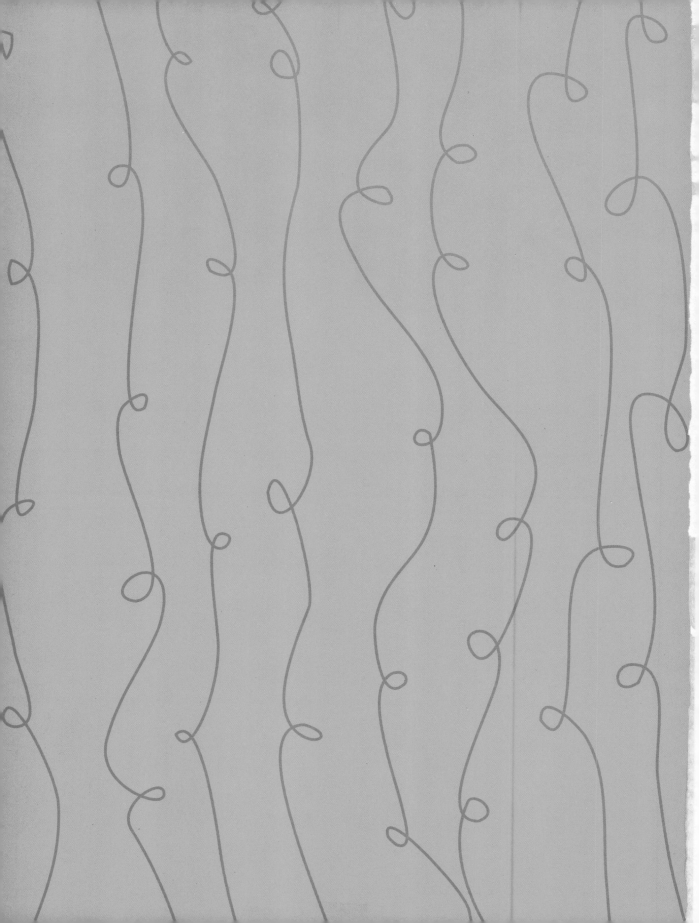

{ the yarn girls' guide to
knits for older kids }

the yarn girls' guide to
knits for older kids

quick-to-knit patterns
for four- to ten-year-olds

JULIE CARLES AND JORDANA JACOBS
PHOTOGRAPHY BY ELLEN SILVERMAN

POTTER CRAFT

NEW YORK

Published in the United States
by Potter Craft, an imprint of the
Crown Publishing Group, a division of
Random House, Inc., New York.
www.crownpublishing.com
www.clarksonpotter.com

POTTER CRAFT and CLARKSON N. POTTER
are trademarks, and POTTER
and colophon are registered trademarks
of Random House, Inc.

Portions of this work previously appeared in
The Yarn Girls' Guide to Beyond the Basics (Potter
Craft, New York, 2005).

Library of Congress
Cataloging-in-Publication Data
is available upon request.

ISBN-10: 0-307-33690-5
ISBN-13: 978-0-307-33690-3

Printed in China

Design by Jennifer K. Beal

10 9 8 7 6 5 4 3 2 1

First Edition

acknowledgments

We want to thank everybody who's been involved in making this book:

All the kids who modeled-Cleo, Jeremy, Andrew, Michael, Ben, Sam, Jesse, Ursula, Jules, Desmond, Lacey, Sela, Shaniqua, Arnelle, Luka, and Bia.

Their parents for taking time out of their busy schedules to bring them to the studio.

Ellen Silverman, for the beautiful photographs, as always.

Christina Holmes for her genius on the computer.

Mercedes Bravo for all the beautiful samples she knit.

Our Yarn Company staff, without whom we truly could not have done this.

Our editors, Rosy Ngo and Elizabeth Wright, and everybody else at Potter Craft who was involved in the making of this book.

Carla Glasser, our great agent.

Daniella Tineo Cohn and Gael Cadden for the illustrations.

And of course all of our customers, who inspire our stories and keep knitting alive.

Contents

introduction

We bought our store, The Yarn Company, almost nine years ago. During that time many, many, many of our customers have had babies. We've seen these babies grow into toddlers and big kids right before our eyes. And we've seen the mothers, grandmothers, and other loved ones who once knit voraciously for their little ones shy away from knitting for them when they got bigger.

Why, we wondered.

We asked around, and people gave us some very valid reasons. First and foremost, they said there are very few books that have simple, stylish patterns for the four- to ten-year-old age group. Second, older kids are a little pickier than babies. They know what they like to wear and the colors they like, and they will refuse to wear something if it isn't soft enough or if it makes them look dorky. Finally, the kids are bigger than they used to be. So, the sweaters that once only took a handful of hours to knit now take twice as much time and twice as much money.

Because of this scarcity of patterns for "big kids," we often write them ourselves. Of course, the more patterns we wrote, the more we realized what a great idea it would be to do a Yarn Girls' book with patterns for children between the ages of four and ten.

And so here it is: A book for older kids full of sweaters and accessories that are casual, stylish, simple, quick to knit, and easy to wear. There are classic designs that will never go out of style like simple pullovers, cardigans, and a great hooded sweatshirt (also known as a "hoodie" by the under-ten set). There are some funky, trendy options such as our marvelous swing coat with fuzzy trim and our poncho with fabulous fringe—both are perfect for the little glamour girls in your life. To keep them warm in the frosty winter months,

we've included patterns for cozy hats and scarves. Finally, there are two super-soft blankets that kids will love to cuddle up with, and two fun pillows that will add a little flair to any room.

We've organized this book in the same way as *The Yarn Girls' Guide to Kid Knits*. One chapter contains three very basic patterns for both pullovers and cardigans, followed by chapters featuring three patterns for these shapes that use slightly more advanced techniques, such as striping, single-row striping, intarsia, and cables. There is also a chapter for V-neck sweaters, in which we've included two pullovers and two cardigans. There is a hat chapter, a scarf chapter, a blanket and pillow chapter, and a "just for girls" chapter, which contains a poncho, a dress, a coat, and a head scarf. As in *Kid Knits*, all patterns (except for those in the girls' chapter) are unisex. To demonstrate this, we have knit up each design in two colorways: one for a boy and one for a girl. The book also provides instructions for all the techniques involved in the patterns, as well as a section of helpful hints to help you avoid any unnecessary pitfalls as you work. Our patterns are clear and concise, and we provide you with step-by-step directions to assist you in shaping armholes and necks.

Like our other books, this one relies on yarns that will knit up relatively quickly. Gauges here range from 5 stitches per inch to 2 stitches per inch. And since kids grow so quickly, the sweater patterns are slightly oversized in the hope that the garments you knit will last more than just one season. But beware, kids' sizes do vary dramatically within this age group. We used measurements that have worked for our customers' kids over the years, but you should look at the finished measurements of the sweater and determine whether they will work for the child for whom you are knitting. For example, if you are making something for a small eight-year-old, it may be better to opt for the 6–7 size option.

Finally, keep in mind that it is not necessary to use the exact yarns we have listed. For the most part, we prefer to use natural fibers, which tend to cost more. But our yarn choices are merely suggestions. If you prefer to use other yarns, just make sure that you are knitting to the required gauge and that you purchase the correct quantity. We provide information about gauge and yardage at the beginning of each pattern. You can also read the Helpful Hints section for more information about substituting yarns.

Our most important advice is to have fun with the book! Get the child you are knitting for involved in the process. Let him or her pick the pattern, the yarn, or colors. If the child is involved with your hobby, you're sure to be happy with the results. The kids will be more likely to wear what you've knit for them, and who knows—you might just be responsible for bringing another generation into the knitting fold. The garter stitch scarf, called *Beginner's Luck,* and the *Half-Hour Hat,* which is a roll hat, are both great beginner projects for any child who wants to learn to knit.

Happy Knitting!
Julie and Jordana

THE VERY BASICS
slip knot and cast on

Even before you begin to knit, you must cast the necessary number of stitches onto your needle.

To do this, you have to measure out a length of yarn for a "tail," which will become your cast-on stitches. The length of the tail determines how many stitches you can cast on; the more stitches you are casting on, the longer the tail must be. Our rule of thumb is that an arm's length—that is, the distance from your wrist to your shoulder—of yarn will yield 20 stitches on the needle.

After you measure out the tail, make a slip knot, which will also be your first cast-on stitch. Place this on a needle, hold that needle in your right hand, and continue to cast on stitches until you have the required number on the needle.

to make a slip knot

1. Measure out the required length of yarn and, with the free end hanging, make a loop at the measured point. You should see an *X*. (Illus. A)

2. Grab hold of the strand of yarn that is on the top of the *X* and bring this strand behind and through the loop. (Illus. B)

3. Hold this new loop in one hand and pull on the loose ends to create your slip knot! (Illus. C & D)

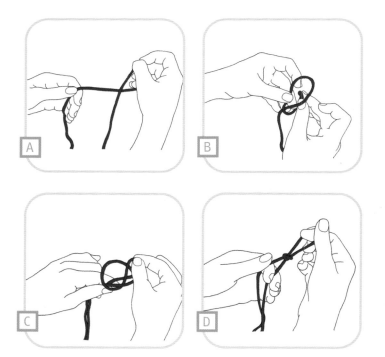

to cast on

1. Place your slip knot on a needle. Hold the needle in your right hand pointing toward the left. Hold the slip knot in place with your right index finger so it does not fly off the needle. (Illus. A)

2. Place the thumb and index finger of your left hand between the 2 strands of yarn dangling from the needle. (Your thumb should be closer to you and the index finger away from you.) Hold the dangling yarn taut with your ring and pinky fingers. (Illus. B)

3. Flip your left thumb up while guiding the needle down and to the left. A loop should form around your thumb. (Illus. C)

4. Guide the needle up through the loop on your thumb. (Illus. D)

5. Guide the needle over the yarn that is around your index finger and catch it with the needle. (Illus. E)

6. Guide the yarn hooked by the needle down through the loop around your thumb. (Illus. F) Slip your thumb out of its loop and place this thumb inside the strand of yarn that is closer to you. Pull down gently. Now you have a cast-on stitch!

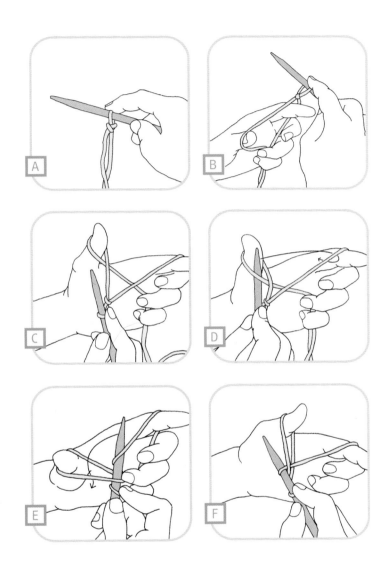

knit and purl

to knit

1. Cast on the desired number of stitches. Hold the needle with the cast-on stitches in your left hand and the empty needle in your right hand. Point the needles toward each other. (Illus. A)

2. While holding the yarn in the back, insert the right needle from front to back through the first stitch on the left needle. You will see that the needles form an *X* with the right needle beneath the left needle. (Illus. B)

3. Keep the needles crossed by holding both needles with the thumb, index, and middle fingers of your left hand. With your right hand, pick up the yarn and wrap it under and around the bottom needle; do not wrap it around the left needle. (Illus. C)

4. Hold the yarn in place around the right needle between your right thumb and index finger and guide the right needle toward you through the center of the stitch on the left needle. (Illus. D) The right needle should now be on top of the left needle. (Illus. E)

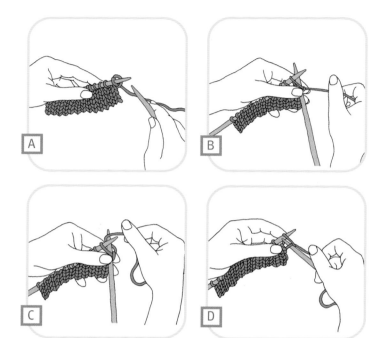

5. Pull the remaining yarn off the left needle by pulling the right needle up and to the right so the newly formed stitch slides off the left needle to the right. You will have a newly created stitch on the right needle. (Illus. F)

6. Repeat steps 1 through 5 across the entire row of stitches.

NOTE:
WHEN YOU FINISH KNITTING THE ENTIRE ROW, ALL OF YOUR STITCHES WILL BE ON THE RIGHT NEEDLE. PLACE THE EMPTY NEEDLE IN YOUR RIGHT HAND AND THE NEEDLE WITH THE STITCHES ON IT IN YOUR LEFT HAND. NOW YOU ARE READY TO BEGIN KNITTING ANOTHER ROW.

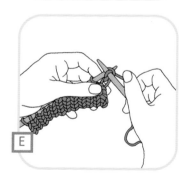

to purl

1. Hold the needle with the stitches in your left hand and the empty needle in your right hand and the loose yarn hanging in front of your work. The needles should be pointed toward each other. (Illus. A)

2. Insert the right needle back to front through the front of the first stitch on the left needle. The needles will form an X with the right needle on top of the left needle. Make sure the yarn is in front of the needle. (Illus. B)

3. Keep the needles crossed in the X position by holding both needles with the thumb, index, and middle fingers of your left hand. Wrap the yarn over and around the front needle from the back, bringing the yarn around and in front of the right needle. (Illus. C)

4. Holding the yarn in place around the needle with the thumb and index finger of your right hand, push the right needle down and toward the back through the center of the stitch on the left needle. (Illus. D) The right needle will now be behind the left needle. (Illus. E)

5. Pull the remaining yarn off the left needle by pulling the right needle to the right so the newly formed stitch slides off the left needle onto the right needle. (Illus. F)

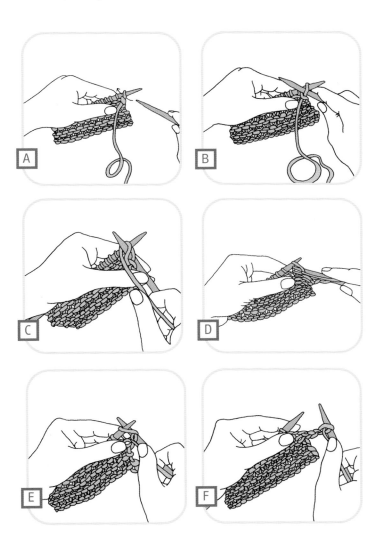

stockinette and garter

Now you know how to knit and purl. If you alternate knitting a row and purling a row, you will be working in the most commonly used stitch, the stockinette stitch. This is universally abbreviated as **St st.** If you just knit or just purl on every row, then you are working in the garter stitch.

knit side

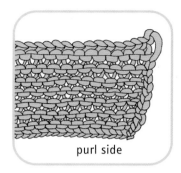

purl side

ribbing

The illustrations here show a Knit 2, Purl 2 ribbing.

to make a ribbing

1. Knit 2 stitches. (Illus. A)

2. Separate the needles slightly and bring the yarn from the back of your work to the front. Be sure you bring the yarn between the needles and not over a needle (which would cause you to add a stitch). (Illus. B)

3. Purl 2 stitches. (Illus. C)

4. After purling, you must bring the yarn between the needles to the back of the work before you knit the next 2 stitches. (Illus. D)

5. Repeat these steps for your ribbing. Note how knit stitches are over knit stitches and purl stitches are over purl stitches. (Illus. E)

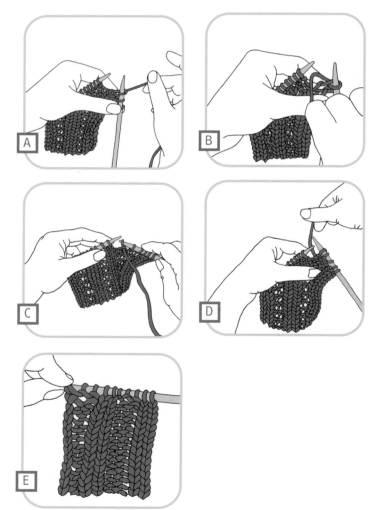

increase and decrease

INCREASING

Increasing is how you will add stitches on a needle in order to add width to your knitted piece.

You will encounter just one method for increasing in this book, which is called the bar method. The bar method, known as Make 1, or **M1,** is our preferred way to increase while knitting sleeves. Generally, we recommend you start a bar increase 2 stitches in from the edge of your work. This means you should knit 2 stitches, then do a bar increase, then knit until there are 2 stitches remaining on the left needle, then increase again. Increasing 2 stitches in from your edge makes sewing up seams much easier because you can sew down a straight line that is uninterrupted by increases.

bar method
(also referred to as make 1, or m1)

1. At the point you wish to add a stitch, pull the needles slightly apart to reveal the bar located between 2 stitches. (See arrow, Illus. A)

2. With your left needle, pick up the bar from behind. (Illus. B)

3. Knit the loop you have made. Be sure to knit this loop as you would normally knit a stitch, going from the front of the stitch to the back. (Illus. C) Sometimes this stitch is a little tight and will be difficult to knit. In that case, gently push the loop up with your left forefinger, loosening the stitch and making it easier to insert your right needle.

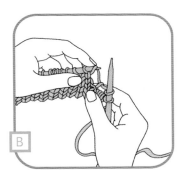

knitting into the front and back of a stitch

1. Begin to knit into the stitch you are going to increase into. Stop when you have brought the right needle through the stitch on the left needle and it is forming the *X* in the front. (Illus. A) DO NOT take the stitch off the left needle as you normally would when completing a knit stitch.

2. Leave the stitch on the left needle and move the tip of the right needle so it is behind the left needle. (Illus. B)

3. Insert the right needle into the back of the stitch on the left needle (Illus. C) and knit it again—wrap yarn under and around the back needle. Hold the yarn against the needle with your right hand and guide the needle toward you through the center of the stitch. The right needle should end up on top of the left needle.

4. Pull the stitch off the left needle. You now have 2 new stitches on the right needle. (Illus. D)

DECREASING

Decreasing is how you will reduce the number of stitches on a needle in order to narrow the width of your knitted piece.

In this book, we use two methods of decreasing. The first is a slip, slip, knit, abbreviated as **SSK.** This is a left-slanting decrease. The other method is a Knit 2 together, abbreviated as **K2tog.** This is a right-slanting decrease.

slip, slip, knit (ssk)

We use this method when we want our decreases to slant toward the *left*.

1. One at a time, slip 2 stitches as though you were going to knit them (knitwise), to the right needle. (Slipping a stitch means that you insert your right needle into the loop on the left needle as though you were going to knit it BUT you don't complete the knit stitch; you just slide the stitch off the left needle onto the right needle.) (Illus. A)

2. Insert the left needle into the front of the 2 slipped stitches, forming an *X*, with the left needle in front of the right needle. (Illus. B)

3. Wrap the yarn under and around the back needle and knit the 2 slipped stitches together, slipping the completed new stitch onto the right needle. (Illus. C & D)

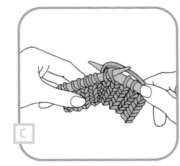

knit 2 together (k2tog)

We use this technique when we want our decreases to slant to the *right*.

1. Working on a knit row, insert your right needle from front to back into the second and then the first stitch you want to knit together. (Illus. A)

2. Bring the yarn around the needle to complete the stitch as with a regular knit stitch. (Illus. B & C)

bind off

Binding off is how you get your knitted piece off the needles and prevent it from unraveling.

1. Knit 2 stitches. (Illus. A)

2. Insert the left needle into the front of the first stitch on the right needle. Using the left needle, pull the first stitch up and over the second stitch. (Illus. B) Place your forefinger on the second stitch to hold it in place and keep it from coming off the needle.

3. Now push that stitch off the left needle completely. (Illus. C & D)

4. Knit one more stitch and repeat the last two steps. Continue this process until you have bound off the desired number of stitches.

When you have finished binding off all your stitches at the end of your work, you should have 1 loop left on the right needle. At this point, cut the yarn, leaving 3 or 4 inches, and pull the end through the remaining loop to tie it off.

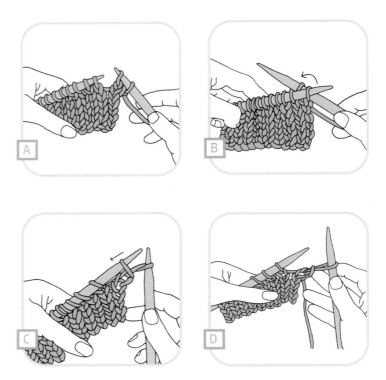

BEYOND BASIC TECHNIQUES
yarn overs

A yarn over (abbreviated **YO**) allows you to make a hole in your knitting on purpose—as opposed to those inadvertent holes made by dropping stitches. Yarn overs are generally used for lace knitting or to make a buttonhole.

yarn over before a knit

If the stitch after the yarn over will be a knit, use this method:

1. Hold both needles with the fingers of your left hand and hold the yarn with your right hand in back of the right needle. (Illus. A)

2. Pull the yarn up and around the right needle from the back to the front to the back again. (Illus. B) You have created the yarn over, which is just a loop.

yarn over before a purl

If the stitch after the yarn over will be a purl, use this method:

1. Hold both needles with the fingers of your left hand and hold the yarn with your right hand in front of the right needle. (Illus. A)

2. Pull the yarn up and around the needle, from the front to the back and to the front again. (Illus. B)

slip stitch

Slipped stitches add interest and texture to a knitted fabric. Although it may sound tricky, making a slip stitch is easier than knitting and purling.

1. Insert the right needle into the stitch on the left needle as if to purl.

2. Move this stitch to the right needle. The yarn will be attached to the stitch preceding the slipped stitch.

color work

We use two types of color work in our patterns. Striping is the easiest way to incorporate different colored yarns into a knitted project. Once your colors are attached (just as simple as starting a new ball of yarn), all you need to do is drop the color you are working with and pick up the color you need to use next. You begin and end a stripe at the beginning of a row. Intarsia is a technique used to add or change color in the middle of a row. For this book, we used only two colors at a time so you don't need to use bobbins (holders for a small amount of yarn); you can use the whole balls of yarn.

multirow striping

1. Work the number of desired rows in color A. Leave the yarn of color A attached. (Illus. A)

2. Add in color B by looping the new yarn around the right needle (Illus. B) and knitting the first stitch.

3. Work the number of desired rows in color B.

4. To switch to color A, let go of color B and pick up color A. (Illus. C & D)

5. Knit with color A for the number of desired rows. (Illus. E)

6. Continue striping until the required length. (Illus. F)

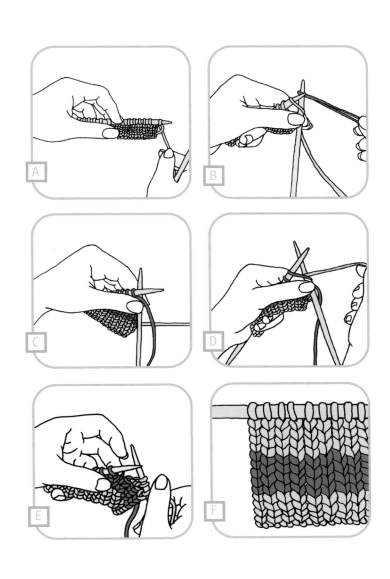

If you are making very wide stripes, you might prefer to cut the yarn each time you switch colors. Otherwise, just leave the unused yarn hanging until it is time to alternate colors.

HELPFUL HINT:
WHEN WORKING IN A STRIPE PATTERN, COUNT THE NUMBER OF STRIPES TO MAKE SURE YOU HAVE KNIT THE SAME NUMBER OF ROWS UP TO THE ARMHOLE AND TO THE TOP OF THE SWEATER.

single-row striping

Unlike the usual technique for making wider stripes, for single row striping you need to work each color over an odd number of rows. This means that your yarn will never be in the correct place to use again unless you cut it and then tie it on at the other end where you need it. Doing that, however, leaves lots of unwanted ends, which will need to be woven in. Our method for single-row striping allows knitters to carry the yarn up their work as they would with even-row striping. This method actually works with any striping that involves an odd number of rows.

NOTE:

YOU CANNOT USE STRAIGHT NEEDLES WHEN EMPLOYING THIS TECHNIQUE; YOU MUST USE CIRCULAR NEEDLES.

1. Knit with color A. (Illus. A)

2. Slide stitches to the right end of the needle. (Illus. B)

3. Knit with color B. (Illus. C)

4. You are now ready to purl. Color A and color B are now at the same end of the needle. (Illus. D)

5. Purl with color A. (Illus. E)

6. Color A and color B are now at different ends of the needle. Slide stitches to the right end of the needle where color B is. (Illus. F)

7. Purl with color B. (Illus. G)

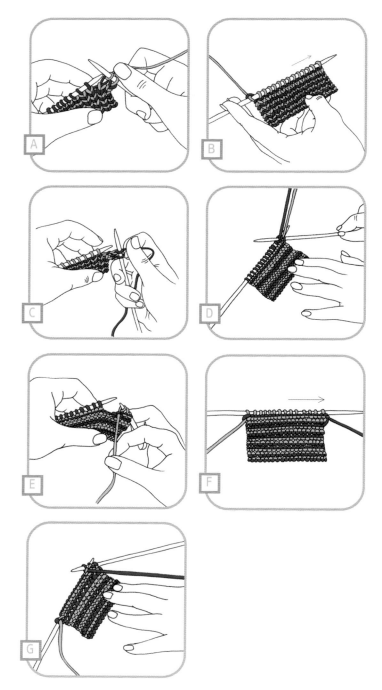

intarsia

1. Cast on the desired number of stitches with color A and color B. (Illus. A)

2. Knit across the stitches of color B, then pick up color A and bring it under color B. (Illus. B)

3. Begin knitting the stitches in color A. (Illus. C)

4. Purl across the stitches of color A. (Illus. D)

5. Pick up color B and bring it under color A and then begin purling the stitches in color B. (Illus. E)

6. This is what the knit side of your work should look like. (Illus. F)

7. This is what the purl side of your work should look like. (Illus. G)

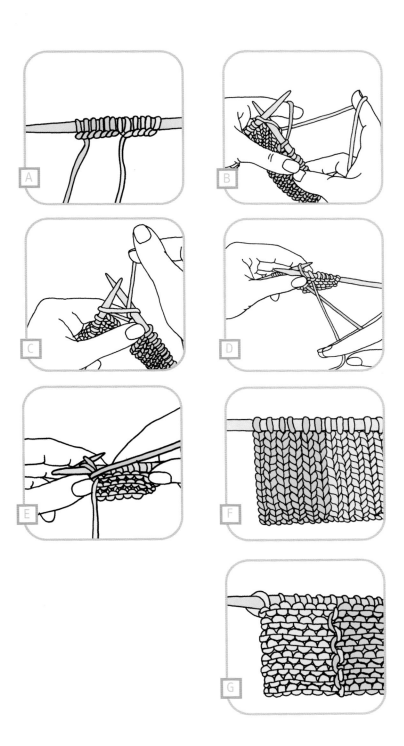

cables

Basically, cables are made by twisting the order of the stitches. Simple or complicated, cables are all based on the same premise: rearranging the stitches on the needle so they cross over to create a twist. To rearrange the order of stitches, you need a cable needle. There are various types of cable needles but they all have the same function. There are J-hooks, metal ones with a bump in the center, and wooden ones that are straight—we personally like the straight wooden ones because wood is generally less slippery than metal and holds the stitches on the cable needle better.

A basic cable stitch pattern reads like this: C8B or C12F. The C stands for cable. The number in the middle denotes the total number of stitches that the cable is worked over. You will divide this number in half to determine how many stitches to put on the cable needle. The B or F stands for back or front and indicates where you will hold the stitches on the cable needle while you are knitting the stitches from the left needle. We tend to like back cables because they can be done without cable needles if you are in a pinch—just pass over the group of stitches that would normally go on the cable needle and knit the required number of stitches from the left needle. Then take the right needle and twist it a little and knit the first stitches. Pull all the stitches off the left needle together.

1. Slip the required number of stitches onto a cable needle, purlwise. Hold these stitches at the back (or front) of the work, as indicated in the pattern. (Illus. A)

2. Knit the required number of stitches off the left needle. (Illus. B)

3. Knit the stitches off the cable needle. (Illus. C)

4. This is what a finished cable will look like. (Illus. D)

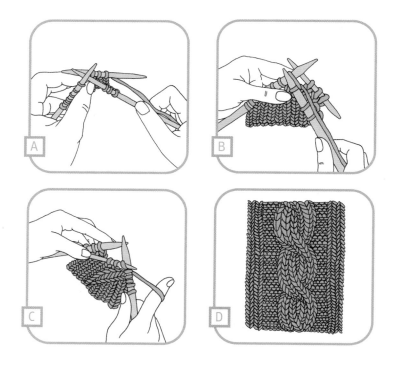

FINISHING TECHNIQUES

You can spend hours knitting row after row of perfect ribbing and flawless stockinette stitch, but all those efforts can be undermined by sloppy finishing technique. Knowing how to sew a sweater together properly is the ultimate key to whether the sweater looks handmade—or homemade. If you use the proper techniques, the process should be relatively painless and your sweater should look virtually seamless. And a final steaming, known as blocking, will smooth over any inconsistencies or bumpy seams.

Some tips:

- Sweaters are always sewn on the right side.

- Although other people might tell you differently, we prefer **not** to use the yarn we knit our sweater with to sew it together. Generally, we suggest using a needlepoint yarn in a similar color because using a different yarn allows you to see what you are doing much more clearly. And, dare we say it, it also enables you to rip out what you have done, if necessary, without inadvertently damaging the sweater itself.

Whether you are making a V-neck, a turtleneck, a crewneck, or a cardigan, sweaters are always assembled in the same order:

1. Sew shoulder seams together.

2. Sew sleeves onto sweater.

3. Sew sleeve seams from armhole to cuff.

4. Sew side seams from armhole to waist.

Once the pieces are joined together, you can add crochet edgings, pick up stitches for a neck, create button bands for a cardigan, or embellish your project with other finishing touches.

sewing side & sleeve seams

1. Cut a piece of yarn approximately twice the length of the sleeve and side seam.

2. Attach the yarn by inserting the sewing needle through the 2 seams at the underarm. Pull the yarn halfway through and make a knot. Half of the yarn should be used to sew the side seam and half should be used to sew the sleeve seam.

3. It doesn't matter whether you start with the body or the sleeve. For both, find the 2 vertical bars 1 full stitch in from the edge and begin the sewing process (Illus. A), taking 2 bars from one side of the sweater and then 2 bars from the other side. (Illus. B) Make sure you are going into the hole where the yarn last came out and pulling the yarn every few stitches. (Illus. C)

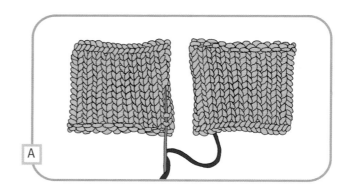

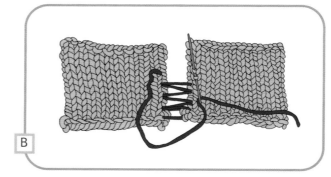

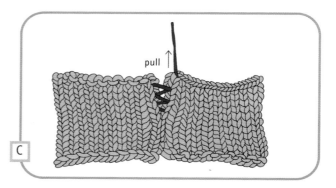

sewing up rolled edges

When sewing up a project that has rolled edges, you will want to finish it so you don't see the seam when the fabric rolls. Start by sewing your seam as you always do, on the right side of the work, BUT at about 1 inch or so before you reach the bottom, you must start sewing on the wrong side of the work instead of the right side. The seam will then show up on the right side, but the rolled edge will cover it.

sewing a raglan sweater together

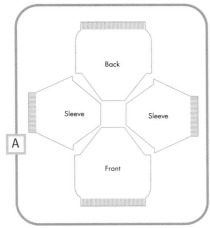

A

Raglan sweaters look intimidating to sew together but they are actually easier than a set-in sleeve because the sleeve seams always fit perfectly since you have knit the same number of rows for all the raglan pieces. The easiest way to begin sewing a raglan sweater together is to place all the pieces flat on a smooth surface so the front and back are opposite each other and the sleeves fit into the armholes on opposite sides. (Illus. A) You will sew all the raglan pieces together first. Start at the armhole and sew up to the neck. You will be sewing a sleeve piece to a body piece each time—there will be 4 seams in total here. Once this is done, fold the sweater in half and sew up the side and sleeve seams as you would on a set-in or drop-sleeve sweater.

weaving in ends

While you are knitting, try to keep your ends about 4 inches long. Remember this when you are adding a new ball of yarn or casting on or binding off. If the ends are long enough, you can weave them in with a sewing needle. All you do is thread the needle with an end and weave the yarn back and forth through the seam 3 to 4 times. Then snip the end. You do not need to make a knot. If the ends are too short, you can use a crochet hook.

blocking

Sometimes when a garment is completely assembled, it requires a bit of shaping. Blocking allows you to reshape the piece gently by applying steam, which relaxes the yarn fibers so they can be stretched in order to smooth out bulky seams, even out uneven knitting, or even enlarge a too-small garment.

Not every piece needs to be blocked; use your common sense. But if you decide reshaping or smoothing is in order, pin your garment onto a padded ironing board, easing it into the desired shape. If your iron can emit a strong stream of steam, hold the iron above the piece without touching it and saturate it with steam. Otherwise, dampen a towel, place it over the garment, and press with a warm iron. Allow the piece to remain pinned to the ironing board until it is completely cool.

Never apply a hot iron directly to a knitted piece, and always read the label on your yarn before blocking; some fibers should not be blocked.

picking up stitches

Once the pieces of your sweater are joined, you need to make nice finished edges and button bands. Rather than knit these elements as separate pieces that are then sewn on, we like to knit them directly onto the finished sweater. In order to do this, you must pick up stitches along the finished edges. When you pick up the stitches for a neck, you are generally picking up stitches horizontally in an already-made stitch. When picking up for button bands, you pick up the stitches vertically, in rows. Either way, the method for picking up the stitches is the same; the difference is where you place the needle to pick up the next stitch. You can pick up stitches in existing stitches (vertically, Illus. A–E) or in rows (horizontally, Illus. F–J).

1. Place the work with the right side facing you. Starting at the right edge of your piece with the knitting needle in your right hand, place the needle in the first stitch, poking through from the outside to the inside. (Illus. A & B; F & G)

2. Loop the yarn under and around the needle and pull the needle back through that same stitch. There should be 1 stitch on the needle. (Illus. C & D; H & I)

3. Continue to poke the needle through each stitch, wrapping the yarn around the needle as if you were knitting and adding a stitch to the needle each time. (Illus. E & J)

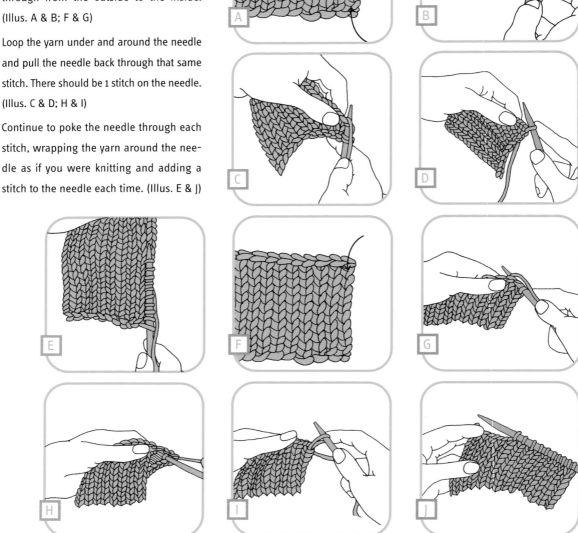

helpful hint

When you are picking up stitches in stitches, as for a crewneck pullover, most of the time you want to pick up every stitch. It is important to note that there is an extra hole between each stitch. So picking up every stitch is the same thing as picking up every other hole. If you poke your needle through every consecutive hole, you will pick up too many stitches.

When you are picking up stitches in rows, as for a button band, you do not want to pick up a stitch in *every* row. To determine how often to pick up, note your gauge. If your gauge is 3 stitches to the inch, then you will want to pick up stitches in 3 consecutive rows, then skip 1 row and repeat this process. If your gauge is 4 stitches to the inch, you will want to pick up stitches in 4 consecutive rows and then skip 1 row. You must skip a row every so often because there are more rows per inch than stitches per inch. If you were to pick up a stitch in every row, when you started to knit these picked-up stitches, you would have too many stitches and the button bands would look wavy.

FINISHING TOUCHES

Fringe, I-cords, and tassels are nice accents on hats, scarves, blankets, and ponchos. Before you begin, you will need a few things. For fringe, you will need a piece of cardboard, a crochet hook, a pair of scissors, and yarn. For an I-cord, you need a circular or double-pointed needle and yarn. For tassels, you need a piece of cardboard, scissors, and yarn.

fringe

To make the fringe, cut a piece of cardboard as tall as the length of fringe you desire. Then wrap the yarn around the cardboard approximately 20 times. (If you need more fringe than this, you can repeat the step.) Cut the strands of yarn across the top of the cardboard. You now have strands of yarn that are twice your desired length. If you want thick fringe, use several strands of yarn; if you want thinner fringe, use only a strand or two.

VERY IMPORTANT:
TO FILL IN THE FRINGE ON A PIECE OF WORK, WE SUGGEST YOU START BY ATTACHING FRINGE AT EACH EDGE AND THEN AT EACH MIDWAY POINT UNTIL YOU ARE SATISFIED.

1. To attach fringe to your knitted garment, insert your crochet hook through a stitch at one of the ends of your knitted piece. You should take the crochet hook from underneath the piece to the top of it, and the crochet hook should be facing you. (Illus. A)

2. Fold your strands of yarn in half and grab the center of these strands with your hook. Pull these strands through the stitch. (Illus. B & C)

3. Remove the crochet hook and place your fingers through the loop you made with the strands of yarn. Then pull the loose ends through this loop. (Illus. D & E)

4. You have completed one fringe. (Illus. F) Even up the ends by trimming them.

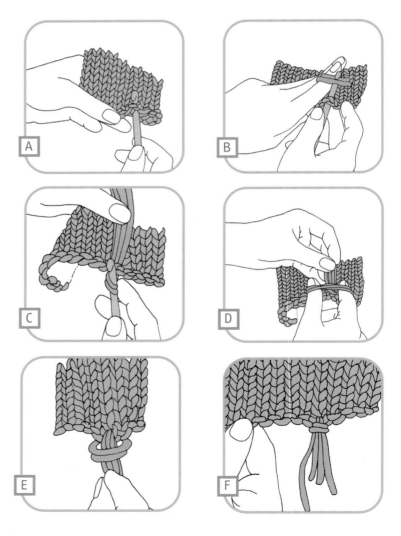

i-cords

You can add I-cords, which are basically knitted ropes, to the top of a hat to add a little pizzazz. They can also be used as purse handles and as cords in a hooded sweatshirt.

1. Using a double-pointed or circular needle, cast on and knit 3 stitches. (Illus. A)

2. Slide these stitches toward the right to the other end of the needle. (Illus. B)

3. Place the needle in your left hand. The yarn will be attached to the stitch far-thest to the left. (Illus. C)

4. Pick the yarn up from behind and knit the 3 stitches. (Illus. D & E)

5. Repeat steps 2–4 until your I-cord reaches the desired length.

6. This is what your I-cord should look like. (Illus. F)

7. To end the I-cord, K3tog, cut the yarn, and pull the tail through the remaining loop to fasten.

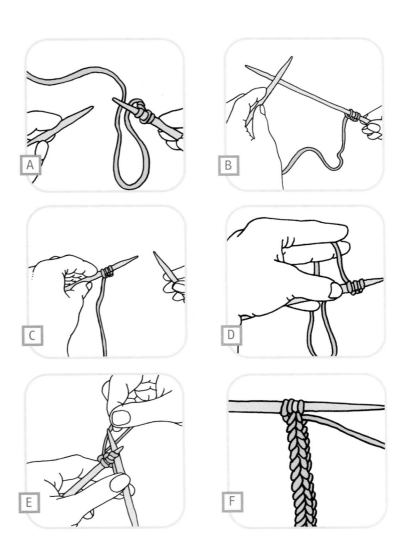

tassels

Tassels are another fun option when adding details to hats. They also look great on a blanket or a poncho.

1. Cut a piece of cardboard a little longer than you want your tassel to be. Wind yarn around the cardboard tightly to desired thickness. (Illus. A)

2. Slide a strand of yarn between the yarn and the cardboard so each loose strand of yarn is on either side. (Illus. B)

3. Tie the strand closed. (Illus. C)

4. Cut the strands of yarn on the bottom end of the cardboard (Illus. D) and remove the cardboard.

5. Tie a strand of yarn around the bundle about 1 inch from the top of the tassel. (Illus. E)

6. Pull this yarn through the center of the top of the tassel and attach to your knitted garment. (Illus. F)

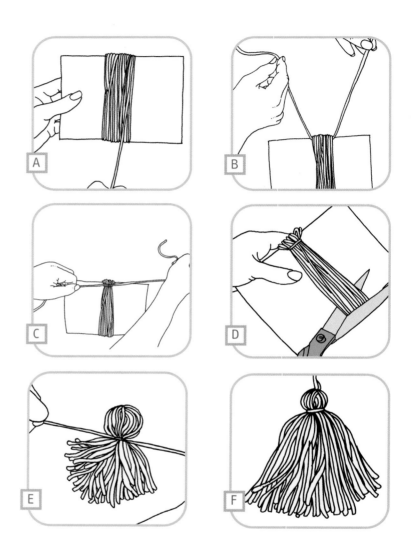

single crochet
and shrimp stitch

Even if you have never crocheted—and never plan to—it's useful to know a couple of basic crochet techniques for finishing off a knitted piece. Crochet edgings give sweaters and throws a nice polished look. Shrimp stitch gives a sturdy corded look. Generally, you want to use a crochet hook that matches the size of the knitting needle you used. For instance, if you used a size 6 knitting needle, you should use a size 6 (also known as size G) crochet hook.

single crochet

1. With the right side of the work facing you, insert your crochet hook through a stitch under the bind-off. (Illus. A)

2. Grab the yarn with the crochet hook and pull it through the stitch to the front of your work. (Illus. B) You will now have 1 loop on the crochet hook. (Illus. C)

3. Insert the crochet hook through the next stitch, hook the yarn, and pull it through the stitch. You now have 2 loops on the crochet hook. (Illus. D & E)

4. Hook the yarn and pull it through both of the loops on the crochet hook. (Illus. F) You will end up with 1 loop on the hook. Insert the hook through the next stitch and repeat across the entire row, ending with 1 loop on the hook.

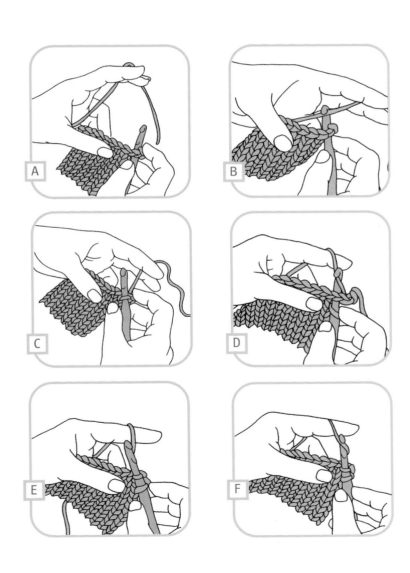

shrimp stitch

This is also known as backwards crochet because you work from left to right instead of right to left. You must do 1 row of single crochet (abbreviated **SC**) before you begin the shrimp stitch.

1. Make a slip stitch by grabbing the yarn through the loop on the hook. (Illus. A)

2. Keeping your right index finger on the loop, insert the hook into the next stitch from the right side to the wrong side of the work. (Illus. B & C)

3. Grab the yarn with the hook and pull it through to the right side of the work. (Illus. D)

4. You should have 2 loops on the hook. (Illus. E)

5. Grab the yarn with the hook and pull it through the 2 loops. (Illus. F & G)

6. Repeat in the next stitch to the right. (Illus. H)

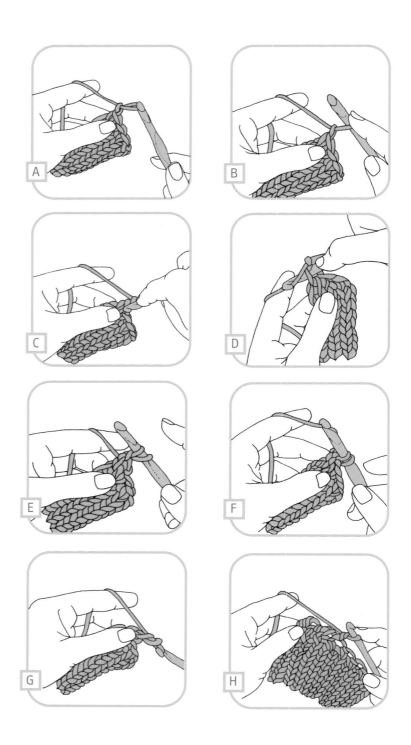

HELPFUL HINTS
make a gauge

THE MOST IMPORTANT MESSAGE IN THIS SECTION IS THAT
YOU MUST ALWAYS MAKE A GAUGE SWATCH!
IF YOU DON'T MAKE A GAUGE SWATCH, THERE ARE NO GUARANTEES THAT YOUR
SWEATER WILL FIT PROPERLY!

It is crucial that you understand gauge. A grasp of gauge will save you the misery of having to rip out your knitting because the sweater you were knitting for your 6-year-old niece looks like it will fit her uncle the football player. And it will help you avoid the depression that comes from investing hours of time on an unwearable garment. If you're not yet a master of gauge, read this information carefully!

STITCH GAUGE = THE NUMBER OF STITCHES REQUIRED TO PRODUCE 1 INCH OF KNITTED FABRIC

Gauge is the most important—and most misunderstood—element of knitting. Simply put, stitch gauge determines the finished measurements of your garment. Technically—and yes, it is a technical, even mathematical concept—stitch gauge tells you the number of stitches you'll need to knit to produce a piece of knitted fabric 1 inch wide.

For each pattern in this book you will find the garment's finished measurements. If your gauge is off, the finished knitted piece will not have the proper dimensions for the size you have chosen. It is, therefore, important to refer to these finished measurements as you knit, making certain your gauge has not changed and that the finished piece will have the correct measurements.

A pattern is always written with a specific gauge in mind, and if you do not get the gauge just right, your project won't turn out as the pattern designer intended.

Here's a simple example: If a pattern says your stitch gauge should be 3 stitches to the inch, that means 60 stitches should produce a piece of knitted fabric 20 inches wide. This is because 60 stitches divided by 3 (your gauge) equals 20 inches. If your gauge were 4 stitches to the inch, you would need to cast on 80 stitches to produce the same 20-inch width.

It really is just that easy: simple division and multiplication, and you can even use a calculator—we do!

All patterns state the stitch gauge (or tension, if it's not an American pattern) required to achieve the desired measurements for your finished garment. The gauge swatch is always knit in the same stitch you'll use for the garment itself. Usually a pattern will tell you that your stitch gauge should be measured over 4 inches (or 10 centimeters if, again, it's not American). For example, under "gauge" your pattern may say "16 stitches = 4 inches." This means that your stitch gauge should be 4 stitches to the inch. Patterns also generally include a row gauge, which indicates how many rows you need to knit in order to get a piece of knitted fabric 1 inch long. For most of the patterns in this book, row gauge is not particularly important, but when knitting a raglan sweater, pay close attention to the row gauge, also.

Along with the gauge, patterns also recommend a needle size to get a particular stitch gauge with a particular yarn. DO NOT assume that just because you are using a pattern's suggested yarn and needle size you don't have to do a gauge swatch. Everybody knits differently. Some people are loose knitters, some are tight knitters, and some are in the middle. Whatever type of knitter you are, you can always get the required gauge eventually, but you may need to make some adjustments. Tight knitters will have to go up in needle size, while loose knitters will have to use needles a size smaller. Remember, it's far more important to get the specified gauge than to use the specified needle—or yarn, for that matter.

Here's how to check your gauge:

- Cast on 4 times the number of stitches required per inch. For example, if the gauge is 4 stitches = 1 inch, cast on 16 stitches; if your gauge is supposed to be 3 stitches = 1 inch, cast on 12 stitches.

- Work in the pattern stitch using the needle size recommended for the body of the sweater. Sometimes ribbing is knit on smaller needles, but you shouldn't use the smaller size for your gauge.

- When your swatch is approximately 4 inches long, slip it off the needle and place it on a flat surface. Measure the width of your swatch. If it measures 4 inches wide, you're getting the required gauge and can begin your knitting project.

- If your swatch is more than 4 inches wide, your knitting is too loose. Reknit your swatch on needles a size or two smaller and measure again. Repeat as necessary, using smaller needles until you get the correct gauge.

- If your swatch is less than 4 inches wide, your knitting is too tight. Reknit your swatch on needles a size or two larger and measure the swatch again. Repeat as necessary, using larger needles until you get the correct gauge.

You should also know that gauge can change as you make your garment. This happens for a multitude of reasons and does not mean you are a bad knitter. Please check the width of what you are knitting once the piece measures about 3 inches long. Compare it to the measurements the pattern provides and make adjustments in the needle size if necessary.

REMEMBER:
Always knit a gauge
swatch—*always!!*

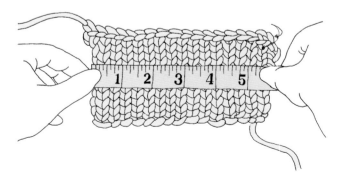

stuff that may help you along the way

We know you want to get to the good stuff—the patterns—but if you read over these helpful hints and keep them in mind as you knit, you might save yourself from ripping out rows of stitches or untangling a gaggle of knots.

using multiple strands of yarn

In some patterns, we used more than one strand of yarn. This means we knit with two or more strands of yarn as though they were one. We did this because we really liked a certain yarn, but it wasn't thick enough as a single strand. To use multiple strands of yarn, you can wind the separate balls into one ball. We find this easier than working from two or more balls at once. You do not need to hold the yarn any differently. Work as though there is one strand. Do not worry if the strands twist.

attaching new yarn when shaping the neck for a pullover

When you have finished binding off one side of a neck on a V-neck or crewneck pullover, you will be instructed to attach the yarn and continue binding off on the other side of the neck. Make sure you attach the yarn in the center of the sweater and not at the outside or shoulder edge.

increasing on sleeves

You can begin to increase on sleeves on the row after the ribbing. If there is a rolled edge, you can begin after 4 rows. When the instructions tell you to increase every 4th row, this means after the first time you increase. You do not need to work 4 rows after the ribbing and then begin to increase.

This is where your increasing should occur on a stockinette sweater where you are increasing every 4th row:

Row 1: Knit—Increase
Row 2: Purl
Row 3: Knit
Row 4: Purl

Repeat rows 1–4 until the required number of increases has been worked.

striping: to cut or carry

When you are striping, you should try to carry your yarn. This means you should not cut the yarn each time you need to use a new color. You will have two or more balls of yarn hanging. If you are using more than two colors, we suggest placing the balls in plastic baggies when you are not using them. The reason to carry the yarn is that sewing the sweater together will be much easier and neater if you do. You will not have tons of ends to weave in. However, there are a few instances when you might want to cut the yarn. The first is if you do not need to use a color again for many inches. The other is if all the balls hanging are driving you mad.

choosing yarn for your sweater

For many knitters, the second most exciting part of a project is picking out the yarn. There are so many delicious new yarns on the market today, in lush colors and irresistible textures, you may feel like a kid in a candy store when you shop for yarn. We do, and we own the candy store!

We have noted the specific yarn we used for each pattern as well as the number of balls we used and the yardage. However, if you can't find the same yarn for any reason—it could be discontinued, or your shop just might not carry it—you can easily substitute yarns, as long as you choose a yarn or combination of yarns that gets the same gauge as the yarn we used.

Also, just because we used double strands of yarn doesn't necessarily mean you must. If you prefer to substitute a yarn that knits to the required gauge using a single strand, that's okay. Just be sure that when you choose a different yarn, you base the amount you will need on the yardage and not on the number of grams or balls. For example, if we use 10 balls of yarn that have 100 yards in each ball and we are knitting with a single strand of yarn, we are using 1,000 yards of yarn. If the yarn you like has 50 yards per ball, you will need 20 balls. Or, if we use 8 balls of a yarn that has 100 yards and we are using a double strand of yarn, we are using 800 yards. But if you want to use a yarn that gets the same gauge with a single strand and it has 80 yards per ball, you will need only 5 balls.

needle size

Needles come in sizes from less than 0 all the way up to 50. Your needle size helps determine your gauge (see Make a Gauge, page 41), and you need to use different size needles with different yarn weights and thicknesses. A size 0 needle has a very small diameter and is used with very, very fine yarns to make tightly textured, fine work, especially for baby clothes. A size 7 needle is a medium-size needle that is generally used with medium-weight yarn. A size 50 needle looks like a turkey baster and is used with incredibly chunky yarn or many strands knitted together at once. This produces a very thick knitted fabric.

reverse shaping

We use this term when we want you to make two pieces, one the mirror image of the other. When you shape the neck on a pullover, you bind off the center stitches and then finish one side of the sweater at a time. On one side you will have to shape the neckline in one direction (while knitting) and on the other side you will have to shape it in the other direction (while purling). Also, when you make a cardigan, you make two front sections—one that will be the right side when worn and one that will be the left side when worn—and must shape the necklines and armholes in opposite directions. The easiest way to visualize this is to shape one side without really thinking about it and then, when you get to the neck shaping on the second side, lay both pieces out as they would be on the finished sweater. You will see what the second neckline needs to look like.

how to tell if you have enough yarn for your project

It stinks to run out of yarn when you are working on the second sleeve of your sweater. Even if you choose the exact yarn and have the same stitch gauge as the pattern indicates, there are times you may need more or less yarn because the particular yarn you are using has a few extra or a few less yards per ball. Even if the difference is just a yard or two per ball, over the course of ten or fifteen balls, the yardage can really add up. Another factor that affects yardage is that your row gauge may be slightly different. If you end up knitting one extra row per every ten rows to get the same measurement as the original knitter, you'll most likely need an extra ball of yarn. Sometimes we have customers who follow our directions but need an extra ball or use one ball less. We know it is a pain to have to run back to the yarn store, but the *real* problem occurs if the specific color or yarn you need is no longer available.

Luckily, if you pay attention to how much yarn you are using as you knit, you can avoid these frustrations. The rule of thumb is that a sweater is broken down into thirds. You use a third of the total amount of yarn needed for the back, a third for the front, and a third for both sleeves. To determine how much yarn you are using, all you have to do is knit a ball and see how far it goes. Then divide the number of inches knit with the one ball into the length of the sweater, and that is a good estimate of how many balls you will need to knit the back. Multiply that number by three and that is how many balls you will need for the entire sweater. If the sweater has a large neck, add one extra ball. Note: A raglan sweater is broken down into quarters.

yardage

Yardage helps you determine how many balls of yarn you will need for your project. Many books and patterns tell you that you need a certain number of grams or ounces, but in our experience this is an inaccurate way to determine the amount of yarn you will need, as different fibers have different weights. Acrylic is a much lighter fiber than wool: A 50-gram ball of acrylic yarn might contain 200 yards, whereas a 50-gram ball of wool might contain only 125 yards. Therefore, if a pattern called for 200 grams of acrylic yarn and you bought 200 grams of wool instead, you would be 300 yards short. In this book, we always specify the total number of yards needed for each pattern.

how to figure out what size to make your sweater

Measure a sweater that fits your child now. If you think that you will knit the sweater up in a jiffy, make it close to that size. If you think it might take you a little time, then make it a little bigger. We generally recommend erring on the bigger size for kids because they are always growing. Oversized garments look cute on kids—they can roll up the sleeves, and if it's a little long, then they will get to wear it even after the growth spurt. If you are knitting for a child that is not yours and you have no access to a sweater, you can always measure a sweater at a kid's store where sizing is universally accepted.

The sweaters in this book are meant to be slightly oversized and the measurements are based on an average child of the given age. When we did our photo shoot, the sweaters fit some of the kids in their age groups perfectly, while others were too big or too small. For example, Jordana's niece, Cleo, is a small eight-year-old, so the 6–7 size garments fit her better than the 8-9. But Desmond, who is seven years old, fit perfectly into the 6-7 garments. So, once again we stress that you should choose the size garment you are going to make based on the sizing and not necessarily on the age.

adjusting sweater measurements

Kids in the four- to ten-year-old age group are all different sizes. Your daughter may have particularly long arms. Your friend's son might have a short torso. And the kid down the block might have an unusually large head. You can make adjustments where necessary with little complication. If you want to make a certain size sweater but would like to either shorten or lengthen the body of the garment, all you have to do is knit more or less BEFORE the armhole shaping instructions. Do not add or take away length at the top of the sweater, as this will cause the armhole to be either too big or too small. Always make length adjustments before the armhole shaping, and make sure that the armhole length remains the same. If you want to adjust the sleeve length, that's easy also—make the adjustment before the cap shaping instructions. If you are shortening the sleeve length, make sure that you will be able to do all the required increases on the sleeve. If you need to change the frequency of the increase to every 4th row instead of every 6th row, then go ahead. And if the hat seems to short, just add length to it before you begin decreasing, or if you want the hat to be shorter, then begin the decreasing an inch before we suggest.

the gauge of a single strand of yarn we have used double or triple

We have used the following yarns doubled in this book. We have been told by readers of our previous books that it would make substituting yarns easier if you knew the gauge of a single strand of the yarns used. So here you go:

Karabella, Aurora Melange—$4^1/_2$ stitches = 1 inch
Rowan, Felted Tweed—6 stitches = 1 inch
Tahki, Cotton Classic—5 stitches = 1 inch
Koigu, KPPPM—7 stitches = 1 inch
Manos del Uruguay—4 stitches = 1 inch
Manos del Uruguay, Cotton Stria—5 stitches = 1 inch
Blue Sky Alpacas, Alpaca—6 stitches = 1 inch
Filatura di Crosa, Zara—5 stitches = 1 inch
GGH, Relax—3 stitches = 1 inch
GGH, Esprit—3 stitches = 1 inch
Crystal Palace, Chenille—4 stitches = 1 inch
Jaeger, Merino DK—5 stitches = 1 inch

KNITTING GLOSSARY

BIND OFF (CAST OFF)
This is the way you get stitches off the needle at the end of a project. Bind off is also a method used to decrease stitches.

CAST ON
This is how you put stitches onto your needle to begin a project.

DEC.
Decrease. This is how you take stitches away once you have begun knitting. We use three methods of decreasing in this book: SSK, K2tog, and double decrease.

GARTER STITCH
Knit every row. But if you are knitting in the round (on a circular needle), then garter stitch means you should knit 1 round and purl the next.

INC.
Increase. This is how you add a stitch onto your needle once you have begun knitting. We use two methods of increasing in this book, a bar increase (Make 1, abbreviated **M1**) and knitting into the front and back of a stitch.

K
Knit.

K2TOG
Knit 2 stitches together. This is a method of decreasing. It slants your decrease toward the right.

P
Purl.

PURLWISE
This means you should move the yarn from one needle to the other as though you were going to purl the next stitch.

REV ST ST
Reverse stockinette stitch. Purl 1 row, knit 1 row, and the purl side is the right side of the garment.

RS
Right side. This is the side that will face out when you are wearing the garment.

SC
Single crochet.

SEED STITCH
Seed stitch is like a messed-up ribbing. As for ribbing, you alternate knitting and purling, but instead of knitting on the knit stitches and purling on the purl stitches to create ribs, you purl over your knit stitches and knit over your purl stitches to create little "seeds."

SSK
Slip, slip, knit. This is a method of decreasing. It slants your decrease toward the left.

ST ST
Stockinette stitch. Knit 1 row, purl 1 row. But if you are knitting in the round (on a circular needle), then St st means you should knit every round.

WS
Wrong side. This is the side that will face in when you are wearing the garment.

YARN DOUBLED
When you knit with the yarn doubled, you are working with 2 strands of yarn held together as though they were 1. Yarn tripled means working with 3 strands of yarn held together. It is no harder to knit with 2 or 3 strands of yarn than it is to knit with 1. When we tell you to use a yarn doubled or tripled, it means the yarn we used for the pattern needed to be thicker than it actually is in order to achieve the proper gauge. If you prefer not to double or triple yarn, try substituting a bulkier yarn that knits to the gauge with a single strand. Just remember that if you use a single strand of yarn where we used 2, you will need only half the yardage to complete the pattern, or one third if the yarn is tripled.

YO
Yarn over. This is how you make a hole in your work (on purpose).

* . . . . . *
In knitting patterns, asterisks are used to indicate that a series of stitches is to be repeated. Repeat only what is between the asterisks, not what is outside of them. For example, **K2, *[K2, P2]* 3 times** means K2, K2, P2, K2, P2, K2, P2. ***K5, K2tog* across row** means that you should K5, K2tog, K5, K2tog, and so on across the whole row.

basic pullovers

A basic pullover sweater is an essential in any child's wardrobe. It's something he or she can combine with a coat for an extra layer of warmth, or wear alone over a shirt on a chilly spring or fall day. Pullovers are great for younger kids, as there are no buttons to deal with. Older kids often wear them over long button-down shirts.

Best of all for knitters, pullovers are a breeze to make. The three pullovers in this chapter are all of the most basic variety. *Camping Out* is a warm, chunky funnel-neck sweater. It is knit on large needles so it works up super quick. Having a funnel neck, rather than a crew neck, means you won't have to do any neck shaping or picking up of stitches. All you have to do to create the funnel neck is bind off stitches at the beginning of two consecutive rows for the shoulders and then continue knitting for the neck. And the sweater has rolled edges, so you simply knit and purl the entire thing. You don't even have to do any ribbing at the bottom! It really is that easy. *Touring the Vineyards* is a raglan pullover that is very simple to shape since the front and back pieces are identical. The raglan shape differs from your everyday set-in sleeve sweater because the armhole decreases are worked up the full length of the sleeve cap. A raglan sweater has no shoulder seams; the sleeve caps become the shoulder. Lastly, *The Juror* is a simple set-in sleeve pullover. It has a K2, P2 ribbing on the bottom of the front and back pieces, as well as on the sleeve bottoms. We threw a stripe in to add some interest and decided a new neckline would be fun.

camping out

YARN: Classic Elite, Tigress (181 yards / 200g ball)
FIBER CONTENT: 100% wool
COLORS:
GIRL VERSION: 7052
BOY VERSION: 7085
AMOUNT: 2 (2, 3, 3) balls
TOTAL YARDAGE: 362 (362, 543, 543) yards
GAUGE: 2 stitches = 1 inch; 8 stitches = 4 inches
NEEDLE SIZE: US #17 (12mm) or size needed to obtain gauge
SIZES: 4–5 (6–7, 8–9, 10+)
KNITTED MEASUREMENTS: Width = 16" (17", 18", 19"), Length = 17" (18", 19", 21"), Sleeve Length = 11½" (12½", 14", 15")

Note: This sweater has rolled edges, the length of the measurements allows for a ½" loss of length due to the rolled edges.

Every year Jennifer takes her niece and nephew camping. They love to sit around the campfire, tell scary stories and roast marshmallows. And no matter what the temperature is during the day, it's always freezing at night. About two weeks before the trip, Jennifer decided to knit warm sweaters for the kids. With such a limited time frame, she came to us in a bit of a panic. We helped her choose very chunky yarn and wrote the simplest pattern for a funnel neck, so there was no neck shaping to worry about and no need to pick up stitches in the finishing. She came in after the trip to report that her sweaters were hits and no one lost any sleep because of the cold . . . just campfire ghost stories.

BACK AND FRONT:

With #17 needle, cast on 32 (34, 36, 38) stitches. Work in St st until piece measures 10½" (11", 11½", 13") from the cast-on edge, ending with a WS row. SHAPE ARMHOLES: Bind off 2 stitches at the beginning of the next 2 rows. Then decrease 1 stitch at each edge, every other row twice until 24 (26, 28, 30) stitches remain. (See step-by-step instructions.) Continue to work in St st until piece measures 17½" (18½", 19½", 21½") from cast-on edge, ending with a WS row. SHAPE FUNNEL NECK: Bind off 5 (6, 6, 7) stitches at beginning of next 2 rows.

(See step-by-step instructions.) Continue to work in St st on 14 (14, 16, 16) stitches for 6 more rows. Bind off all stitches loosely.

SLEEVES:

With #17 needle, cast on 16 (16, 18, 18) stitches. Work in St st. **AT THE SAME TIME,** increase 1 stitch at each edge, every 6th row 5 (6, 6, 7) times until you have 26 (28, 30, 32) stitches.

Note: Increase leaving 2 edge stitches on either side of work. This means you should knit 2 stitches, increase 1 stitch, knit to the last 2 stitches, increase 1 stitch, and then knit the remaining 2 stitches. Increasing like this makes it easier to sew up your seams.

When sleeve measures 12" (13", 14½", 15½") from cast-on edge, end with a WS row. SHAPE CAP: Bind off 2 stitches at the beginning of the next 2 rows. Then decrease 1 stitch at each edge, every other row twice. Bind off 2 stitches at the beginning of the next 6 (8, 8, 10) rows until 6 (4, 6, 4) stitches remain. Bind off all stitches loosely.

FINISHING:

Sew shoulder seams together. Sew sleeves on. Sew up side and sleeve seams.

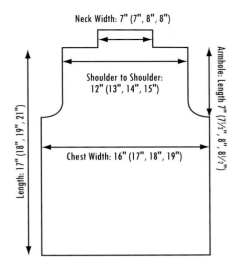

Neck Width: 7" (7", 8", 8")

Shoulder to Shoulder: 12" (13", 14", 15")

Armhole: Length 7" (7½", 8", 8½")

Length: 17" (18", 19", 21")

Chest Width: 16" (17", 18", 19")

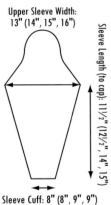

Upper Sleeve Width: 13" (14", 15", 16")

Sleeve Length (to cap): 11½" (12½", 14", 15")

Sleeve Cuff: 8" (8", 9", 9")

STEP-BY-STEP GUIDE TO SHAPING THE ARMHOLES

ROW 1 (RS): Bind off 2 stitches. Knit to end of row.

ROW 2: Bind off 2 stitches. Purl to end of row.

ROW 3: K2, SSK, knit to last 4 stitches, K2tog, K2.

ROW 4: Purl.

Repeat rows 3 and 4 once more.

STEP-BY-STEP GUIDE TO SHAPING THE FUNNEL NECK

ROW 1 (RS): Bind off 5 (6, 6, 7) stitches. Knit to end of row.

ROW 2: Bind off 5 (6, 6, 7) stitches. Purl to end of row.

Continue to work in St st on remaining 14 (14, 16, 16) stitches for 6 more rows. Bind off all stitches loosely.

touring the vineyards

YARN: Karabella, Aurora Melange
(98 yards / 50g ball)
FIBER CONTENT: 100% extrafine
merino wool
COLORS:
GIRL VERSION: 13
BOY VERSION: 4
AMOUNT: 8 (10, 10, 12) balls
TOTAL YARDAGE: 784 (980, 980, 1,176)
yards
STITCH GAUGE: 3 stitches = 1 inch;
12 stitches = 4 inches
ROW GAUGE: 4 rows = 1 inch; 16 rows =
4 inches
NEEDLE SIZE: US #11 (8mm) or size
needed to obtain gauge
SIZES: 4–5 (6–7, 8–9, 10+)
KNITTED MEASUREMENTS: Width = 16"
(17", 18", 19"), Length = 17" (18", 19", 21"),
Sleeve Length = 11½" (12½", 14", 15")

*Yarn is worked double throughout the
sweater—this means you should hold
2 strands of yarn together as though
they are 1. *

Note: This sweater has rolled edges, so
the length of the measurements allows
for a ½" loss.

Jordana and her husband, Jeff, recently went on a romantic and intoxicating trip to Napa for a long weekend. They left their two-year-old son, Max, at home with his grandparents. They had a great time seeing all the vineyards and tasting all the wine. However, we all know how hard it is being away from our young children—Jordana missed Max terribly. So while Jeff drove from vineyard to vineyard, Jordana poured her energy and her heart into knitting this sweater for Max. Come Sunday night, not only did Max get his parents back but he had this fabulous new sweater to wear on Monday. It was so cute, we decided to size it up for bigger kids.

BACK AND FRONT:

With #11 needle and 2 strands of yarn, cast on 48 (52, 54, 58) stitches. Work in St st until piece measures 10½" (10½", 11", 13") from cast-on edge, ending with a WS row. SHAPE RAGLAN ARMHOLES: Bind off 2 stitches at the beginning of the next 2 rows. Then decrease 1 stitch at each edge, every other row 14 (15, 16, 17) times until 16 (18, 18, 20) stitches remain. (See step-by-step instructions.) Work 6 more rows in St st with no further decreasing. Bind off all stitches loosely.

SLEEVES:

With #11 needle and 2 strands of yarn, cast on 22 (24, 26, 28) stitches. Work in St st. **AT THE SAME TIME,** increase 1 stitch at each edge, every 6th row 5 (8, 9, 9) times and then every 4th row 3 (0, 0, 0) times until you have 38 (40, 44, 46) stitches.

Note: Increase leaving 2 edge stitches on either side of work. This means you should knit 2 stitches, increase 1 stitch, knit to the last 2 stitches, increase 1 stitch, and then knit the remaining 2 stitches. Increasing like this makes it easier to sew up your seams.

Continue in St st until sleeve measures 12" (13", 14½", 15½") from cast-on edge, ending with a WS row. SHAPE RAGLAN SLEEVE: Bind off 2 stitches at the beginning of the next 2 rows. Then decrease 1 stitch at each edge, every other row 14 (15, 16, 17) times until 6 (6, 8, 8) stitches remain. Work 6 more rows in St st with no further decreasing. Bind off all stitches loosely.

FINISHING:

Lay all pieces on a flat surface. Sew up raglan seams. Sew up side and sleeve seams.

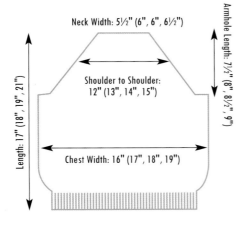

Neck Width: 5½" (6", 6", 6½")

Armhole Length: 7½" (8", 8½", 9")

Shoulder to Shoulder: 12" (13", 14", 15")

Length: 17" (18", 19", 21")

Chest Width: 16" (17", 18", 19")

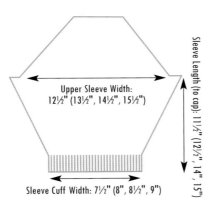

Upper Sleeve Width: 12½" (13½", 14½", 15½")

Sleeve Length (to cap): 11½" (12½", 14", 15")

Sleeve Cuff Width: 7½" (8", 8½", 9")

ROW 1 (RS): Bind off 2 stitches. Knit to end of row.

ROW 2: Bind off 2 stitches. Purl to end of row.

ROW 3: K2, SSK, knit to last 4 stitches, K2tog, K2.

ROW 4: Purl.

Repeat rows 3 and 4 13 (14, 15, 16) more times. Work 6 more rows in St st. Bind off remaining stitches loosely.

the juror

YARN: Rowan, Felted Tweed (191 yards / 50g ball)
FIBER CONTENT: 50% merino wool / 25% alpaca / 25% viscose
COLORS:
GIRL VERSION: A-150, B-142
BOY VERSION: A-154, B-133
AMOUNT: 6 (6, 7, 8) balls color A; 1 (1, 1, 1) ball color B
TOTAL YARDAGE: 1,146 (1,146, 1,337, 1,528) yards color A; 191 (191, 191, 191) yards color B
GAUGE: 4 stitches = 1 inch; 16 stitches = 4 inches
NEEDLE SIZE: US #10 (6mm) or size needed to obtain gauge; US #9 (5.5mm) for ribbing; H/8 (5mm) crochet hook
SIZES: 4–5 (6–7, 8–9, 10+)
KNITTED MEASUREMENTS: Width = 16" (17", 18", 19"), Length = 17" (18", 19", 21"), Sleeve Length = 11½" (12½", 14", 15")
OTHER MATERIALS: 1 zipper

*Yarn is worked double throughout the sweater—this means you should hold 2 strands of yarn together as though they are 1. *

Lisa's eight-year-old niece, Taylor, had been hounding her to knit her a sweater with a stripe. But Lisa had been very busy with work and other obligations. She came in to see us one day, looking rundown and tired. With a jury duty summons in her hand and a smile on her face, she proclaimed, "I will finally have some time to sit down and knit Taylor's sweater." She knew it needed to have a stripe, as per Taylor's request, but she wanted it to be a little different. So we came up with the idea of a polo collar with a zipper. It is very easy to slip on and off and it has a fun, rugged look. And after three days, Lisa was finished not only with the sweater but with her civic responsibility as well.

BACK:

With #9 needle and 2 strands of **color A,** cast on 64 (68, 72, 76) stitches. Work in K2, P2 ribbing for 10 rows as follows: K2, P2 every row. Change to #10 needle and work in St st until piece measures 8½" (9½", 10½", 12") from the cast-on edge, ending with a WS row. Change to 2 strands of **color B** and work 4 rows. Change to 2 strands of **color A** and work until piece measures 10" (10½", 11", 12½") from the cast-on edge, ending with a WS row. SHAPE ARM-HOLES: Bind off 3 stitches at the beginning of the next 2 rows. Bind off 2 stitches at the beginning of the following 2 rows. Then decrease 1 stitch at each edge, every other row 3 times until 48 (52, 56, 60) stitches remain. (See step-by-step instructions.) Continue to work in St st until piece measures 17" (18", 19", 21") from cast-on edge, ending with a WS row. Bind off all stitches loosely.

FRONT:

Work as for back until piece measures 8½" (9½", 10½", 12") from cast-on edge, ending with a WS row. (Work stripe as for Back. Continue in St st until piece measures 10" (10½", 11", 12½").)
SHAPE ARMHOLES: Bind off 3 stitches at the beginning of the next 2 rows. Bind off 2 stitches at the beginning of the following 2 rows. Then decrease 1 stitch at each edge, every other row 3 times until 48 (52, 56, 60) stitches remain. (See step-by-step instructions.) **AT THE SAME TIME,** when piece measures 10½" (11½", 12", 13½") from cast-on edge, ending with a WS row. SHAPE PLACKET: Bind off center 2 stitches. Work 23 (25, 27, 29)

stitches of each side of the neck separately until piece measures 15" (16", 16½", 18½") from cast-on edge, ending with a WS row for the right side and an RS row for the left side. S H A P E N E C K : At beginning of each neck edge, every other row, bind off 4 stitches once, 3 stitches once, 2 stitches once, 1 stitch 2 (2, 3, 3) times. (See step-by-step instructions.) Continue to work on remaining 12 (14, 15, 17) stitches with no further decreasing until piece measures 17" (18", 19", 21") from cast-on edge, ending with a WS row. Bind off all stitches loosely.

SLEEVES:

With #9 needle and 2 strands of **color A,** cast on 32 (34, 36, 36) stitches. Work in K2, P2 ribbing for 10 rows as follows: For 4–5, 8–9, and 10+ sizes: K2, P2 every row. For 6–7 size: **Row 1 (RS):** K2, (*P2, K2*) to end. **Row 2:** P2, (*K2, P2*) to end. Repeat rows 1 and 2 4 times more. Change to #10 needle and work in St st. **AT THE SAME TIME,** increase one stitch at each edge every 4th row 9 (10, 11, 12) times until you have 50 (54, 58, 60) stitches.

Note: Increase leaving 2 edge stitches on either side of work. This means you should knit 2 stitches, increase 1 stitch, knit to the last 2 stitches, increase 1 stitch, and then knit the remaining 2 stitches. Increasing like this makes it easier to sew up your seams.

When sleeve measures 11½" (12½", 14", 15") from cast-on edge, end with a WS row. S H A P E C A P : Bind off 3 stitches at the beginning of the next 2 rows. Bind off 2 stitches at the beginning of the following 2 rows. Then decrease 1 stitch at each edge, every other row 3 times. Bind off 2 stitches at the beginning of the next 14 (16, 16, 18) rows until 6 (6, 10, 8) stitches remain. Bind off remaining stitches loosely.

FINISHING:

Sew shoulder seams together. Sew sleeves on. Sew up side and sleeve seams. With a #9 needle and 2 strands of **color A,** pick up 56 (56, 60, 60) stitches around neck and work in K2, P2 ribbing for 2". Change to 2 strands of **color B.** Work 1 row of rib and then bind off all stitches loosely. With an H/8 crochet hook, work 1 row single crochet and 1 row shrimp stitch up each side of placket. Sew in zipper.

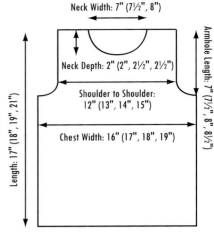

Neck Width: 7" (7½", 8")
Neck Depth: 2" (2", 2½", 2½")
Shoulder to Shoulder: 12" (13", 14", 15")
Chest Width: 16" (17", 18", 19")
Armhole Length: 7" (7½", 8", 8½")
Length: 17" (18", 19", 21")

Upper Sleeve Width: 12½" (13½", 14½", 15")
Sleeve Length (to cap): 11½" (12½", 14", 15")
Sleeve Cuff Width: 7" (7½", 8", 8")

STEP-BY-STEP GUIDE TO SHAPING THE ARMHOLES

ROW 1 (RS): Bind off 3 stitches. Knit to end of row.
ROW 2: Bind off 3 stitches. Purl to end of row.
ROW 3: Bind off 2 stitches. Knit to end of row.
ROW 4: Bind off 2 stitches. Purl to end of row.
ROW 5: K2, SSK, knit to last 4 stitches, K2tog, K2.
ROW 6: Purl.

Repeat rows 5 and 6 2 more times.

STEP-BY-STEP GUIDE TO BINDING OFF THE CENTER STITCHES

Remember that after binding off the center stitches, you will work one side at a time.

ROW 1 (RS): Pattern 25 (27, 29, 31) stitches; with the 24th (26th, 28th, 30th) stitch, begin to bind off the center 2 stitches. For example, for the 4–5 size, this means you should pull the 24th stitch over the 25th stitch, and this is your first bind-off. When you are done binding off the center 2 stitches, check to make sure you have 23 (25, 27, 29) stitches on each side of the hole, including the stitch on the right-hand needle. Knit to end of row. Turn work.
ROW 2: Purl.
ROW 3: Knit.

Repeat rows 2 and 3 (working on the right side only) until piece measures 15" (16", 16½", 18½") from cast-on edge, ending with a WS row.

STEP-BY-STEP GUIDE TO SHAPING THE CREW NECK

RIGHT FRONT
(right side when worn)

ROW 1 (RS): Bind off 4 stitches. Knit to end of row.
ROW 2: Purl.
ROW 3: Bind off 3 stitches. Knit to end of row.
ROW 4: Purl.
ROW 5: Bind off 2 stitches. Knit to end of row.
ROW 6: Purl.
ROW 7: Bind off 1 stitch. Knit to end of row.
ROW 8: Purl.

Repeat rows 7 and 8 1 (1, 2, 2) more times. Continue in St st until piece measures 17" (18", 19", 21") from cast-on edge, ending with a WS row. Bind off all stitches loosely.

Attach 2 strands of yarn to the remaining stitches at the center of the work (not at the outside edge). Work in St st on left front until piece measures 15" (16", 16½", 18½") from cast-on edge, ending with a RS row.

LEFT FRONT
(left side when worn)

ROW 1 (WS): Bind off 4 stitches. Purl to end of row.
ROW 2: Knit.
ROW 3: Bind off 3 stitches. Purl to end of row.
ROW 4: Knit.
ROW 5: Bind off 2 stitches. Purl to end of row.
ROW 6: Knit.
ROW 7: Bind off 1 stitch. Purl to end of row.
ROW 8: Knit.

beyond basic pullovers

The three pullover sweaters in this chapter will take you one step beyond the simple stockinette sweater. Each pattern includes a new little something, so if you are a beginner, you can try out a new technique with each sweater you knit.

Riding the Rails introduces a skill called intarsia. Intarsia is a colorwork method in which blocks of color are worked with separate balls of yarn. This sweater is one of the simplest intarsia patterns you will find because it uses only two colors at a time and the color changes are worked in a straight vertical line. Although this method is easy to master, it makes the sweater itself extra special with different colors but no stripes. *Waste Not, Want Not* is a striped sweater, but this is not your everyday striped sweater: each stripe is just one row of a color. To make a single-stripe sweater you need to work on a circular needle, then slide your stitches to the appropriate end of your needle in order to find the color yarn you need to pick up. It is a fun process, and the numerous stripe colors allow you to create a sweater that goes with many outfits. *Down Under* is a cable and rib sweater. It introduces you to the basic cable technique. A cable is just a simple twist, made by using a cable needle. You place some stitches onto the cable needle, knit some from your left-hand needle, and then knit the stitches from the cable needle. That is all there is to it. It's really a very easy sweater to knit, yet everyone who sees it will ooh and aah over how complicated it looks.

riding the rails

YARN: Tahki, Cotton Classic (108 yards / 50g ball)
FIBER CONTENT: 100% mercerized cotton
COLORS:
GIRL VERSION: A-3412, B-3540
BOY VERSION: A-3039, B-3885
AMOUNT: 6 (7, 8, 9) balls color A; 3 (4, 4, 5) balls color B
TOTAL YARDAGE: 648 (756, 864, 972) yards color A; 324 (432, 432, 540) yards color B
GAUGE: 3$\frac{1}{2}$ stitches = 1 inch; 14 stitches = 4 inches
NEEDLE SIZE: US #10$\frac{1}{2}$ (6.5mm) or size needed to obtain gauge; circular 16" US #10.5 (6.5mm) for neck edging
SIZES: 4–5 (6–7, 8–9, 10+)
KNITTED MEASUREMENTS: Width = 16" (17", 18", 19"), Length = 17" (18", 19", 21"), Sleeve Length = 11$\frac{1}{2}$" (12$\frac{1}{2}$", 14", 15")

*Yarn is worked double throughout the sweater—this means you should hold 2 strands of yarn together as though they are 1. *

Jessica has always lived and worked in New York City. So when her company moved to a town an hour away, she found herself doing the reverse commute. She looked on the bright side; with her new train ride came an extra two hours of knitting time each day. Jessica had a ton of gifts she wanted to knit for her friends' kids and she resolved to make them sweaters during her commute. She wanted to learn intarsia, so we helped her design this four-quadrant pullover. This project is a great way to begin intarsia, and since she was only using two colors it was also very portable.

BACK:

With #10$\frac{1}{2}$ needle and 2 strands of **color A,** cast on 56 (60, 64, 66) stitches. Work in St st as follows: **Row 1 (RS):** K28 (30, 32, 33) stitches with **color A** and K28 (30, 32, 33) stitches with 2 strands of **color B. Row 2:** P28 (30, 32, 33) stitches with **color B** and P28 (30, 32, 33) stitches with **color A.** Continue to work in established pattern with **color A** and **color B** until piece measures 8$\frac{1}{2}$" (9", 9$\frac{1}{2}$", 10$\frac{1}{2}$") from the cast-on edge, ending with a WS row. Then work in St st as follows: **Row 1:** K28 (30, 32, 33) with **color B** and K28 (30, 32, 33) with **color A. Row 2:** P28 (30, 32, 33) stitches with **color A** and

P28 (30, 32, 33) stitches with **color B.** Continue to work in established color pattern until piece measures 10" (10$\frac{1}{2}$", 11", 12$\frac{1}{2}$") from cast-on edge. SHAPE ARMHOLES: Bind off 3 stitches at the beginning of the next 2 rows. Bind off 2 stitches at the beginning of the following 2 rows. Then decrease 1 stitch at each edge, every other row twice until 42 (46, 50, 52) stitches remain. (See step-by-step instructions.) Continue to work in St st until piece measures 17" (18", 19", 21") from cast-on edge, ending with a WS row. Bind off all stitches loosely.

FRONT:

Work as for back until piece measures 10" (10$\frac{1}{2}$", 11", 12$\frac{1}{2}$") from cast-on edge, ending with a WS row. SHAPE ARMHOLES: Bind off 3 stitches at the beginning of the next 2 rows. Bind off 2 stitches at the beginning of the following 2 rows. Then decrease 1 stitch at each edge, every other row twice until 42 (46, 50, 52) stitches remain. (See step-by-step instructions.) Continue to work in St st until piece measures 14$\frac{1}{2}$" (15$\frac{1}{2}$", 16$\frac{1}{2}$", 18$\frac{1}{2}$") from cast-on edge, ending with a WS row. SHAPE CREW NECK: Bind off center 12 (14, 14, 14) stitches and then begin working each side of the neck

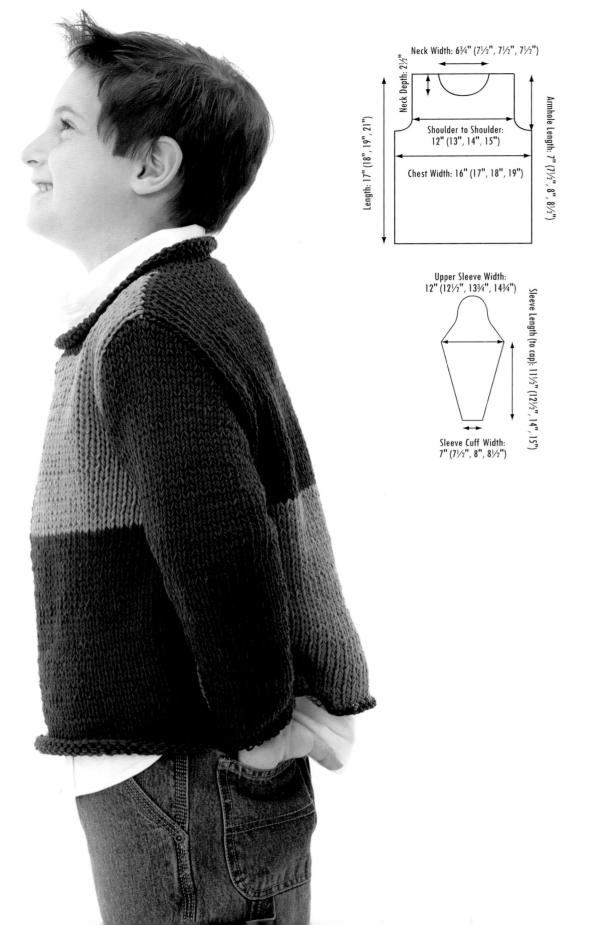

Neck Width: 6¾" (7½", 7½", 7½")

Neck Depth: 2½"

Length: 17" (18", 19", 21")

Armhole Length: 7" (7½", 8", 8½")

Shoulder to Shoulder: 12" (13", 14", 15")

Chest Width: 16" (17", 18", 19")

Upper Sleeve Width: 12" (12½", 13¾", 14¾")

Sleeve Length (to cap): 11½" (12½", 14", 15")

Sleeve Cuff Width: 7" (7½", 8", 8½")

separately. At the beginning of each neck edge, every other row, bind off 3 stitches once, 2 stitches once, 1 stitch once. (See step-by-step instructions.) Continue to work on remaining 9 (10, 12, 13) stitches with no further decreasing until piece measures 17" (18", 19", 21") from cast-on edge, ending with a WS row. Bind off all stitches loosely.

SLEEVES:

With #10½ needle and 2 strands of **color A,** cast on 24 (26, 28, 30) stitches. Work in St st. **AT THE SAME TIME,** increase one stitch at each edge every 6th row 9

(9, 10, 11) times until you have 42 (44, 48, 52) stitches.

Note: Increase leaving 2 edge stitches on either side of work. This means you should knit 2 stitches, increase 1 stitch, knit to the last 2 stitches, increase 1 stitch, and then knit the remaining 2 stitches. Increasing like this makes it easier to sew up your seams.

When sleeve measures 11½" (12½", 14", 15") from cast-on edge, end with a WS row. SHAPE CAP: Bind off 3 stitches at the beginning of the next 2 rows. Bind off 2 stitches at the beginning of the next 2 rows. Then decrease 1 stitch at each edge, every other row once. Bind

off 2 stitches at the beginning of the next 10 (10, 12, 14) rows until 10 (12, 12, 12) stitches remain. Bind all stitches loosely.

FINISHING:

Sew shoulder seams together. Sew sleeves on and then sew up side and sleeve seams. With a circular 16" #10½ needle and 2 strands of **color A,** pick up 62 (64, 64, 66) stitches around neck and work in St st for 6 rows. Bind off all stitches loosely.

STEP-BY-STEP GUIDE TO SHAPING THE ARMHOLES

ROW 1 (RS): Bind off 3 stitches. Knit to end of row.
ROW 2: Bind off 3 stitches. Purl to end of row.
ROW 3: Bind off 2 stitches. Knit to end of row.
ROW 4: Bind off 2 stitches. Purl to end of row.
ROW 5: K2, SSK, knit to last 4 stitches, K2tog, K2.
ROW 6: Purl.
Repeat rows 5 and 6 once more.

STEP-BY-STEP GUIDE TO SHAPING THE CREW NECK

Remember that after binding off the center stitches, you will work one side at a time.
ROW 1 (RS): Pattern 17 (18, 20, 21) stitches; with the 16th (17th, 19th, 20th) stitch begin to bind off the center 12 (14, 14, 14) stitches. For example, for the 4–5 size, this means you should pull the 16th stitch over the 17th stitch, and this is your first bind-off. When you are done binding off the center 12 (14, 14, 14) stitches, check to make sure you have 15 (16, 18, 19) stitches on each side of the hole, including the stitch on the right-hand needle. Knit to end of row. Turn work.
ROW 2: Purl.
ROW 3: Bind off 3 stitches. Knit to end of row.
ROW 4: Purl.
ROW 5: Bind off 2 stitches. Knit to end of row.
ROW 6: Purl.
ROW 7: Bind off 1 stitch. Knit to end of row.
ROW 8: Purl.

* When you are done with the bind-off instructions, compare the length of the front piece to the length of the back. If the front and back measure the same, bind off the remaining stitches. If the front is too short, continue knitting and purling until the pieces are of equal length, then bind off all stitches loosely.
* For the other side of the neck edge, attach yarn to the remaining stitches at the center of the work (not at the side edge) and begin binding off stitches immediately. You will now be binding off with a WS row facing you. Finish neck shaping as on other side, but purling to the end of the row and knitting the even numbered rows. Bind off remaining stitches loosely.

waste not, want not

YARN: Debbie Blis, Cashmerino Aran (95 yards / 50g ball)

FIBER CONTENT: 55% merino wool / 33% microfibre / 12% cashmere

COLORS:

GIRL VERSION: A-603, B-611, C-602, D-617, E-102

BOY VERSION: A-207, B-102, C-502, D-205, E-300

AMOUNT: 2 (2, 3, 3) balls color A; 2 (2, 3, 3) balls color B; 2 (2, 3, 3) balls color C; 2 (3, 3, 3) balls color D; 2 (2, 3, 3) balls color E

TOTAL YARDAGE: 190 (190, 285, 285) yards color A; 190 (190, 285, 285) yards color B; 190 (190, 285, 285) yards color C; 190 (285, 285, 285) yards color D; 190 (190, 285, 285) yards color E

GAUGE: 4½ stitches = 1 inch; 18 stitches = 4 inches

NEEDLE SIZE: US #9 (5.5mm) or size needed to obtain gauge; US #8 (5mm) for ribbing; circular 16" US #8 (5mm) for neck ribbing

SIZES: 4–5 (6–7, 8–9, 10+)

KNITTED MEASUREMENTS: Width = 16" (17", 18", 19"), Length = 17" (18", 19", 21"), Sleeve Length = 11½" (12½", 14", 15")

In one of our previous books, *The Yarn Girls' Guide to Beyond the Basics*, we knit a cardigan with the single-stripe method using multiple colors. Julie was wearing that sweater the day Roz came in. Roz wanted to knit a fun, yet practical sweater for her granddaughter, and she also wanted to learn something new. After pouring through many pattern books, Roz still couldn't find anything she was crazy about, so Julie suggested making a smaller version of the sweater she had on. Roz smiled and said, "Why didn't you suggest that before I wasted my time looking through all those books? I love it, but how about making it as a pullover?" She chose some fun colors and then sat down and learned the simple technique.

Note: When you begin armhole shaping you cannot carry the yarn over all rows. You will need to cut and reattach the yarn when needed. You will not be using the single-stripe method of sliding the yarn back and forth. Once you finish the armhole decreases you can continue in the single-stripe method. This is also the case for the neck shaping. (See page 22 for the single-stripe technique.)

STRIPED ST ST:

1 row A

1 row B

1 row A

1 row D

1 row C

1 row E

1 row C

1 row D

1 row B

1 row A

1 row B

1 row D

1 row E

1 row C

1 row E

1 row D

BACK:

With #8 needle and **color D,** cast on 72 (76, 82, 86) stitches. Work in seed stitch ribbing for 6 rows as follows: **Row 1 (RS):** K1, P1. **Row 2:** P1, K1. Change to #9 needle and work in Striped St st until piece measures 10" (10½", 11", 12½")

from cast-on edge, ending with a WS row. SHAPE ARMHOLES: Bind off 3 stitches at the beginning of the next 2 rows. Bind off 2 stitches at the beginning of the following 2 rows. Then decrease 1 stitch at each edge, every other row 4 (4, 5, 5) times until 54 (58, 62, 66) stitches remain. (See step-by-step instructions.) Continue working in Striped St st until piece measures 17" (18", 19", 21") from cast-on edge, ending with a WS row. Bind off all stitches loosely.

FRONT:

Work as for back until piece measures 10" (10½", 11", 12½") from cast-on edge, ending with a WS row. SHAPE ARMHOLES: Bind off 3 stitches at the beginning of the next 2 rows. Bind off 2 stitches at the beginning of the following 2 rows. Then decrease 1 stitch at each edge, every other row 4 (4, 5, 5) times until 54 (58, 62, 66) stitches remain. (See step-by-step instructions.) Continue working in Striped St st until piece measures 14½" (15½", 16½", 18½") from cast-on edge, ending with a WS row. SHAPE CREW NECK: Bind off center 16 (18, 18, 20) stitches and then begin working each side of the neck separately. At the beginning of each neck edge, every other row, bind off 3 stitches once, 2 stitches once, 1 stitch twice. (See step-by-step instructions.) Continue to work on remaining 12 (13, 15, 16) stitches with no further decreasing until piece measures 17" (18", 19", 21") from cast-on edge, ending with a WS row. Bind off all stitches loosely.

SLEEVES:

With #8 needle and **color D,** cast on 34 (36, 38, 40) stitches. Work in seed stitch ribbing for 6 rows as follows: **Row 1 (RS):** K1, P1. Row 2: P1, K1. Change to #9 needle and work in Striped St st. **AT THE SAME TIME,** increase one stitch at each edge every 6th row 9 (10, 11, 12) times until you have 52 (56, 60, 64) stitches.

Note: Increase leaving 2 edge stitches on either side of work. This means you should knit 2 stitches, increase 1 stitch, knit to the last 2 stitches, increase 1 stitch, and then knit the remaining 2 stitches. Increasing like this makes it easier to sew up your seams.

When sleeve measures 11½" (12½", 14", 15") from cast-on edge, end with a WS row. SHAPE CAP: Bind off 3 stitches at the beginning of the next 2 rows. Bind off 2 stitches at the beginning of the next 2 rows. Then decrease 1 stitch at each edge, every other row 4 (4, 5, 5) times. Bind off 2 stitches at the beginning of the next 14 (16, 16, 18) rows until 6 (6, 8, 8) stitches remain. Bind off all stitches loosely.

FINISHING:

Sew shoulder seams together. Sew sleeves on and then sew up side and sleeve seams. With a circular 16" #8 needle, RS facing and **color D,** pick up 79 (83, 83, 85) stitches around the neck and work in seed stitch ribbing for 6 rows as follows: K1, P1 every row. Bind off all stitches loosely.

STEP-BY-STEP GUIDE TO SHAPING THE ARMHOLES

ROW 1 (RS): Bind off 3 stitches. Knit to end of row.

ROW 2: Bind off 3 stitches. Purl to end of row.

ROW 3: Bind off 2 stitches. Knit to end of row.

ROW 4: Bind off 2 stitches. Purl to end of row.

ROW 5: K2, SSK, knit to last 4 stitches, K2tog, K2.

ROW 6: Purl.

Repeat rows 5 and 6 3 (3, 4, 4) more times.

STEP-BY-STEP GUIDE TO SHAPING THE CREW NECK

Remember that after binding off the center stitches, you will work one side at a time.

ROW 1 (RS): Pattern 21 (22, 24, 25) stitches; with the 20th (21st, 23rd, 24th) stitch begin to bind off the center 16 (18, 18, 20) stitches. For example, for the 4–5 size, this means you should pull the 20th stitch over the 21st stitch, and this is your first bind-off. When you are done binding off the center 16 (18, 18, 20) stitches, check to make sure you have 19 (20, 22, 23) stitches on each side of the hole, including the stitch on the right-hand needle. Knit to end of row. Turn work.

ROW 2: Purl.

ROW 3: Bind off 3 stitches. Knit to end of row.

ROW 4: Purl.

ROW 5: Bind off 2 stitches. Knit to end of row.

ROW 6: Purl.

ROW 7: Bind off 1 stitch. Knit to end of row.

ROW 8: Purl.

Repeat rows 7 and 8 once more.

* When you are done with the bind-off instructions, compare the length of the front piece to the length of the back. If the front and back measure the same, bind off the remaining stitches loosely. If the front is too short, continue working in Striped St st until the pieces are of equal length, then bind off all stitches loosely.

* For the other side of the neck edge, attach yarn to the remaining stitches at the center of the work (not at the side edge) and begin binding off stitches immediately. You will now be binding off with a WS row facing you. Finish neck shaping as on other side, but purling to the end of the row and knitting the even numbered rows. Bind off remaining stitches.

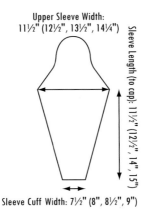

Upper Sleeve Width: 11½" (12½", 13½", 14¼")

Sleeve Length (to cap): 11½" (12½", 14", 15")

Sleeve Cuff Width: 7½" (8", 8½", 9")

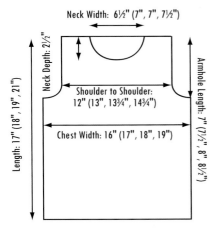

Neck Width: 6½" (7", 7", 7½")

Neck Depth: 2½"

Shoulder to Shoulder: 12" (13", 13¾", 14¾")

Length: 17" (18", 19", 21")

Armhole Length: 7" (7½", 8", 8½")

Chest Width: 16" (17", 18", 19")

down under

YARN: GGH, Savanna (85 yards / 50g ball)
FIBER CONTENT: 43% alpaca / 23% linen / 19% wool / 15% nylon
COLORS:
GIRL VERSION: 22
BOY VERSION: 16
AMOUNT: 7 (8, 9, 10) balls
TOTAL YARDAGE: 595 (680, 765, 850) yards
GAUGE: 3$\frac{1}{2}$ stitches = 1 inch; 14 stitches = 4 inches in St st
NEEDLE SIZE: US #10$\frac{1}{2}$ (6.5mm) or size needed to obtain gauge; circular 16" US #10 (6mm) for neck ribbing; cable needle
SIZES: 4–5 (6–7, 8–9, 10+)
KNITTED MEASUREMENTS: Width = 16" (17", 18", 19"), Length = 17" (18", 19", 21"), Sleeve Length = 11$\frac{1}{2}$" (12$\frac{1}{2}$", 14", 15")

Suzanne, the Yarn Company manager, has a sister, Alisa, who lives in Australia. Whenever she goes to visit her, Suzanne spends a lot of time planning two projects to take with her. Project #1 is always a simple stockinette or garter project that she can knit during the movies. Project #2 requires a little more concentration, for when she can work her mind and her hands at the same time. She decided this cable and rib pattern would be the perfect second project for her trip. Between two knitting projects, a few naps, and a few movies, she was Down Under before she knew it.

PATTERN STITCH:

C8B = place 4 stitches on a cable needle, hold at back of the work, knit 4 stitches from the left-hand needle, knit 4 stitches from the cable needle.

BACK:

With #10$\frac{1}{2}$ needle, cast on 60 (68, 76, 84) stitches. Work in pattern as follows:

ROW 1 (RS): [K2, P2] 2 (3, 4, 5) times, *K8, [P2, K2] twice, P2*. Repeat from * to * once more, end K8, [P2, K2] 2 (3, 4, 5) times.

ROW 2 (WS): [P2, K2] 2 (3, 4, 5) times, *P8, [K2, P2] twice, K2*. Repeat from * to * once more, end P8, [K2, P2] 2 (3, 4, 5) times.

ROW 3: Repeat row 1.
ROW 4: Repeat row 2.
ROW 5: [K2, P2] 2 (3, 4, 5) times, *C8B, [P2, K2] twice, P2*. Repeat from * to * twice, end C8B, [P2, K2] 2 (3, 4, 5) times.
ROWS 6 AND 8: Repeat row 2.
ROW 7: Repeat row 1.

Continue in this pattern, repeating rows 1–8, until piece measures 10" (10$\frac{1}{2}$", 11", 12$\frac{1}{2}$") from cast-on edge, ending with a WS row. SHAPE ARMHOLES: Bind off 3 stitches at the beginning of the next 2 rows. Bind off 2 stitches at the beginning of the following 2 rows. Then decrease 1 stitch at each edge, every other row 1 (2, 3, 4) times until 48 (54, 60, 66) stitches remain. (See step-by-step instructions.) Continue to work in pattern stitch until piece measures 17" (18", 19", 21") from cast-on edge, ending with a WS row. Bind off all stitches loosely.

FRONT:

Work as for back until piece measures 10" (10$\frac{1}{2}$", 11", 12$\frac{1}{2}$") from cast-on edge, ending with a WS row. SHAPE ARMHOLES: Bind off 3 stitches at the beginning of the next 2 rows. Bind off 2 stitches times at the beginning of the following 2 rows. Then decrease 1 stitch at each edge, every other row 1 (2, 3, 4) times until 48 (54, 60, 66) stitches remain. (See step-by-step instructions.) Continue to work in pattern stitch until piece measures 14$\frac{1}{2}$" (15$\frac{1}{2}$", 16$\frac{1}{2}$", 18$\frac{1}{2}$") from cast-on edge, ending with a

WS row. SHAPE CREW NECK:
Bind off center 8 (10, 10, 12) stitches and
then begin working each side of the
neck separately. At the beginning of
each neck edge, every other row, bind
off 3 stitches once, 2 stitches once, 1
stitch once. (See step-by-step instructions.) Continue to work on remaining
14 (16, 19, 21) stitches with no further
decreasing until piece measures 17" (18",
19", 21") from cast-on edge, ending with
a WS row. Bind off all stitches loosely.

SLEEVES:

With #10½ needle, cast on 24 (26, 28,
30) stitches. Set up rib pattern as follows:

Size 4–5:

ROW 1 (RS): [K2, P2] twice, K8, [P2, K2]
twice.
ROW 2: [P2, K2] twice, P8, [K2, P2] twice.
Size 6–7:
ROW 1 (RS): P1, [K2, P2] twice, K8, [P2,
K2] twice, P1.
ROW 2: K1, [P2, K2] twice, P8, [K2, P2]
twice, K1.
Size 8–9:
ROW 1 (RS): P2, [K2, P2] twice, K8, [P2,
K2] twice, P2.
ROW 2: K2, [P2, K2] twice, P8, [K2, P2]
twice, K2.
Size 10+:
ROW 1 (RS): K1, P2, [K2, P2] twice, K8, [P2,
K2] twice, P2, K1.
ROW 2: P1, K2, [P2, K2] twice, P8, [K2, P2]
twice, K2, P1.
Work in rib/cable pattern, cabling every
8th row as for back and front. **AT THE
SAME TIME,** increase 1 stitch at each
edge, every 4th row 13 (14, 15, 16) times
until you have 50 (54, 58, 62) stitches,
taking increased stitches into the K2, P2
ribbing.

*Note: Increase leaving 2 edge stitches
on either side of work. This means you
should knit 2 stitches, increase 1 stitch,
knit to the last 2 stitches, increase 1
stitch, and then knit the remaining 2
stitches. Increasing like this makes it
easier to sew up your seams.*

When sleeve measures 11½" (12½", 14",
15") from cast-on edge, end with a WS
row. SHAPE CAP: Bind off 3 stitches
at the beginning of the next 2 rows.
Bind off 2 stitches at the beginning of
the next 2 rows. Then decrease 1 stitch
at each edge, every other row 1 (2, 3, 4)
times. Bind off 2 stitches at the beginning of the next 14 (16, 16, 16) rows until
10 (8, 10, 12) stitches remain. Bind off all
stitches loosely.

FINISHING:

Sew shoulder seams together. Sew
sleeves on. Sew up side and sleeve
seams. With a circular 16" #10 needle,
pick up 60 (60, 64, 64) stitches around
neck and work in K2, P2 ribbing for 6
rows. Bind off all stitches loosely.

STEP-BY-STEP GUIDE TO SHAPING THE ARMHOLES

ROW 1 (RS): Bind off 3 stitches. Knit to end of row.

ROW 2: Bind off 3 stitches. Purl to end of row.

ROW 3: Bind off 2 stitches. Knit to end of row.

ROW 4: Bind off 2 stitches. Purl to end of row.

ROW 5: K2, SSK, knit to last 4 stitches, K2tog, K2.

ROW 6: Purl.

Repeat rows 5 and 6 0 (1, 2, 3) more times.

STEP-BY-STEP GUIDE TO SHAPING THE CREW NECK

Remember that after binding off the center stitches, you will work one side at a time.

ROW 1 (RS): Pattern 22 (24, 27, 29) stitches; with the 21st (23rd, 26th, 28th) stitch begin to bind off the center 8 (10, 10, 12) stitches. For example, for the 4–5 size, this means you should pull the 21st stitch over the 22nd stitch, and this is your first bind-off. When you are done binding off the center 8 (10, 10, 12) stitches, check to make sure you have 20 (22, 25, 27) stitches on each side of the hole, including the stitch on the right-hand needle. Knit to end of row. Turn work.

ROW 2: Purl.

ROW 3: Bind off 3 stitches. Knit to end of row.

ROW 4: Purl.

ROW 5: Bind off 2 stitches. Knit to end of row.

ROW 6: Purl.

ROW 7: Bind off 1 stitch. Knit to end of row.

ROW 8: Purl.

* When you are done with the bind-off instructions, compare the length of the front piece to the length of the back. If the front and back measure the same, bind off the remaining stitches loosely. If the front is too short, continue knitting and purling until the pieces are of equal length, then bind off all stitches loosely.

* For the other side of the neck edge, attach yarn to the remaining stitches at the center of the work (not at the side edge) and begin binding off stitches immediately. You will now be binding off with a WS row facing you. Finish neck shaping as on other side, but purling to the end of the row and knitting the even numbered rows. Bind off remaining stitches loosely.

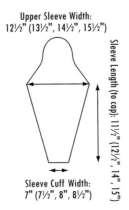

Upper Sleeve Width: 12½" (13½", 14½", 15½")

Sleeve Length (to cap): 11½" (12½", 14", 15")

Sleeve Cuff Width: 7" (7½", 8", 8½")

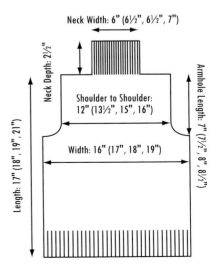

Neck Width: 6" (6½", 6½", 7")

Neck Depth: 2½"

Shoulder to Shoulder: 12" (13½", 15", 16")

Armhole Length: 7" (7½", 8", 8½")

Width: 16" (17", 18", 19")

Length: 17" (18", 19", 21")

basic cardigans

Kids always seem to be inside one minute, outside the next, and then back inside ten minutes later. They eat breakfast in their cozy kitchens, go outside to wait for the school bus, get on the bus, get off the bus, go into school, go outside for recess, go back inside for class, go outside for lunch . . . you get the idea. That's why cardigans are great for kids. They are easy to throw on, then off, then on again. And best of all, when thrown off, a cardigan can easily be wrapped around a child's waist so as not to be lost or forgotten.

The three cardigans in this chapter are all very rudimentary. *Don't Curb Your Enthusiasm* is your most basic style. There is a K1, P1 ribbing on all edges that is knit in one color, and then you simply straight knit a row and purl a row throughout in a second color. This sweater is made with a super chunky yarn that will knit up lickety split. *First Day of School* is also a very straightforward cardigan. We added a little interest to this most basic style by choosing a contrasting color for the button bands and yet another one for the collar. The large collar also makes this sweater a little different from the norm. *Supersize Me* is a great sweater for the kid who always wants to wear sweatshirts. Basically it is a sweat-er/sweatshirt. It has a hood and a zipper, and is big and comfy. What kid could argue with that?

don't curb your enthusiasm

YARN: Tahki, Baby (60 yards / 100g ball)
FIBER CONTENT: 100% merino wool
COLORS:
GIRL VERSION: A-48, B-20
BOY VERSION: A-22, B-14
AMOUNT: 2 (2, 2, 2) balls color A; 4 (5, 6, 7) balls color B
TOTAL YARDAGE: 120 (120, 120, 120) yards color A; 240 (300, 360, 420) yards color B
GAUGE: 2 stitches = 1 inch; 8 stitches = 4 inches
NEEDLE SIZE: US #15 (10mm) for body or size needed to obtain gauge; US #13 (9mm) for neck and button band ribbing
SIZES: 4–5 (6–7, 8–9, 10+)
KNITTED MEASUREMENTS: Width = 16" (17", 18", 19"), Length =17" (18", 19", 21"), Sleeve Length = 11½" (12½", 14", 15")
OTHER MATERIALS: 5 buttons

One of our most excited new knitters is Jonah. He is eight years old and learned to knit at an after-school program. He loves knitting, and we're always happy to see him when he comes into the store because his enthusiasm is infectious and he is just so sweet. After having knit a few hats and scarves, he decided that he wanted to make his four-year-old sister a sweater. We suggested that he use a chunky yarn and knit the borders in a contrasting color to add a little zip but no more difficulty. When he came in about a month later with all of the pieces completed, he could barely contain his excitement. We put the sweater together for him and now his sister wears it every day.

BACK:

With #13 needle and **color A,** cast on 32 (34, 36, 38) stitches. Work in K1, P1 ribbing for 6 rows. Then change to #15 needle and **color B** and work in St st until piece measures 9½" (10", 10½", 12") from cast-on edge, ending with a WS row. SHAPE ARMHOLES: Bind off 2 stitches at the beginning of the next 2 rows. Then decrease 1 stitch at each edge, every other row twice until 24 (26, 28, 30) stitches remain. (See step-by-step instructions.) Continue to work in St st until piece measures 17" (18", 19", 21") from cast-on edge, ending with a WS row. Bind off all stitches loosely.

FRONT:
(make 2, reverse shaping)

With #13 needle and **color A,** cast on 16 (17, 18, 19) stitches. Work in K1, P1 ribbing as follows for 6 rows: For 4–5 and 8–9 sizes: K1, P1 every row. For 6–7 and 10+ sizes: **Row 1 (RS):** K1, *P1, K1*. **Row 2:** P1, *K1, P1*. Change to #15 needle and **color B** and work in St st until piece measures 9½" (10", 10½", 12")

from cast-on edge, ending with a WS row for the left front and a RS row for the right front. SHAPE ARMHOLES AS FOR BACK AT OUTSIDE EDGE ONLY until 12 (13, 14, 15) stitches remain. (See step-by-step instructions.) Continue to work in St st until piece measures 14¹/₂" (15¹/₂", 16¹/₂", 18¹/₂") from cast-on edge, ending with a RS row for the left front and a WS row for the right front. SHAPE CREW NECK: At beginning of neck edge, every other row, bind off 3 stitches once, 2 stitches once, 1 stitch 1 (1, 2, 2) times. (See step-by-step instructions.) Continue to work in St st on remaining 6 (7, 7, 8) stitches until piece measures 17" (18", 19", 21") from cast-on edge ending with a WS row. Bind off all stitches loosely.

SLEEVES:

With #13 needle and **color A,** cast on 16 (16, 18, 18) stitches. Work in K1, P1 ribbing for 6 rows. Change to #15 needle and **color B** and work in St st. **AT THE SAME TIME,** increase 1 stitch at each edge, every 6th row 4 (5, 5, 6) times until you have 24 (26, 28, 30) stitches.

Note: Increase leaving 2 edge stitches on either side of work. This means you should knit 2 stitches, increase 1 stitch, knit to the last 2 stitches, increase 1 stitch, and then knit the remaining 2 stitches. Increasing like this makes it easier to sew up your seams.

When sleeve measures 11¹/₂" (12¹/₂", 14", 15") from cast-on edge, end with a WS row. SHAPE CAP: Bind off 2 stitches at the beginning of the next 2 rows. Then decrease 1 stitch at each edge, every other row twice. Bind off 2 stitches at the beginning of the next 6 (6, 8, 8) rows until 4 (6, 4, 6) stitches remain. Bind off all stitches loosely.

FINISHING:

Sew shoulder seams together. Sew sleeves on. Sew up side and sleeve seams.

NECKBAND:
With #13 needle, **color A,** and RS facing, pick up 32 (32, 34, 34) stitches around the neck. Work in K1, P1 ribbing for 4 rows. Bind off all stitches loosely.

Note: Buttonholes are placed on the right side for girls and the left side for boys.

BUTTON BAND: (This is the left side when made for a girl, and right side when made for a boy.) With #13 needle, **color A,** and RS facing, pick up 38 (40, 44, 48) stitches. Work in K1, P1 ribbing for 4 rows. Bind off all stitches loosely.

BUTTONHOLE BAND: (This is the right side when made for a girl, and left side when made for a boy.) With #13 needle, **color A,** and RS facing, pick up 38 (40, 42, 46) stitches. **Row 1:** K1, P1 ribbing.
Row 2: Rib 2 (3, 2, 2), *YO, Rib2tog, Rib 6 (6, 7, 8)*. Repeat from * to * 3 more times, end YO, Rib2tog, Rib 2 (3, 2, 2).
Rows 3 and 4: K1, P1 ribbing. Bind off all stitches loosely. Sew on buttons.

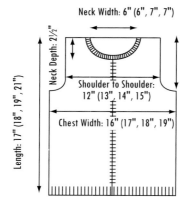

Neck Width: 6" (6", 7", 7")

Neck Depth: 2¹/₂"

Length: 17" (18", 19", 21")

Shoulder to Shoulder: 12" (13", 14", 15")

Chest Width: 16" (17", 18", 19")

Armhole Length: 7¹/₂" (8", 8¹/₂", 9")

BACK

ROW 1 (RS): Bind off 2 stitches. Knit to end of row.
ROW 2: Bind off 2 stitches. Purl to end of row.
ROW 3: K2, SSK, knit to last 4 stitches, K2tog, K2.
ROW 4: Purl.
Repeat rows 3 and 4 once more.

LEFT FRONT

(left side when worn)

(You will be binding off on a RS row)
ROW 1 (RS): Bind off 2 stitches. Knit to end of row.
ROW 2: Purl.
ROW 3: K2, SSK, knit to end of row.
ROW 4: Purl.
Repeat rows 3 and 4 once more.

RIGHT FRONT

(right side when worn)

(You will be binding off on a WS row)
ROW 1 (WS): Bind off 2 stitches. Purl to end of row.
ROW 2: Knit to last 4 stitches, K2tog, K2.
ROW 3: Purl.
Repeat rows 2 and 3 once more.

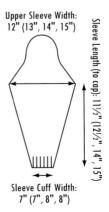

Upper Sleeve Width:
12" (13", 14", 15")

Sleeve Length (to cap): 11½" (12½", 14", 15")

Sleeve Cuff Width:
7" (7", 8", 8")

LEFT FRONT

(left side when worn)

ROW 1 (WS): Bind off 3 stitches. Purl to end of row.
ROW 2: Knit.
ROW 3: Bind off 2 stitches. Purl to end of row.
ROW 4: Knit.
ROW 5: Bind off 1 stitch. Purl to end of row.
ROW 6: Knit.
Repeat rows 5 and 6 0 (0, 1, 1) more time.

RIGHT FRONT

(right side when worn)

ROW 1 (RS): Bind off 3 stitches. Knit to end of row.
ROW 2: Purl.
ROW 3: Bind off 2 stitches. Knit to end of row.
ROW 4: Purl.
ROW 5: Bind off 1 stitch. Knit to end of row.
ROW 6: Purl.
Repeat rows 5 and 6 0 (0, 1, 1) more time.

* When you are done with the bind-off instructions, compare the length of the front piece to the length of the back. If the front and back measure the same, bind off the remaining stitches loosely. If the front is too short, continue knitting and purling until the pieces are of equal length, then bind off all stitches loosely.

first day of school

YARN: Karabella, Aurora Bulky (56 yards / 50g ball)
FIBER CONTENT: 100% extrafine merino wool
COLORS:
GIRL VERSION: A-19, B-28, C-15
BOY VERSION: A-29, B-27, C-24
AMOUNT: 8 (10, 12, 14) balls color A; 1 (1, 1, 1) ball color B; 1 (1, 1, 2) ball(s) color C
TOTAL YARDAGE: 448 (560, 672, 784) yards color A; 56 (56, 56, 56) yards color B; 56 (56, 56, 112) yards color C
GAUGE: 3½ stitches = 1 inch; 14 stitches = 4 inches
NEEDLE SIZE: US #10½ (6.5mm) FOR BODY or size needed to obtain gauge; US #9 (5.5mm) for neck and button band ribbing
SIZES: 4–5 (6–7, 8–9, 10+)
KNITTED MEASUREMENTS: Width = 16" (17", 18", 19"); Length =17" (18", 19", 21"); Sleeve Length = 11½" (12½", 14", 15")
OTHER MATERIALS: 5 buttons

Sara's son, Sam, was very nervous about starting first grade. Every time he thought about it he cried, and Sara felt awful for him. So Sara came up with a plan: She wasn't sure it was going to work, but she hoped it would at least make Sam feel a little better. She told him she was going to knit him a "first day of school sweater" and he could pick whatever colors and style he wanted. She told him that when he wore it on the first day of school it would remind him that she was thinking of him all day long. Both Sam and Sara cried a bit when Sara left on that first day, but when school let out, Sam ran toward Sara, hugged her, and said, "Mom, I liked school. I won't cry tomorrow."

BACK:

With #9 needle and **color A,** cast on 56 (60, 64, 68) stitches. Work in K2, P2 ribbing for 6 rows as follows: K2, P2 every row. Change to #10½ needle and work in St st until piece measures 10" (10½", 11", 12½") from cast-on edge, ending with a WS row. SHAPE ARMHOLES: Bind off 3 stitches at the beginning of the next 2 rows. Bind off 2 stitches at the beginning of the next 2 rows. Then decrease 1 stitch at each edge, every other row twice until 42 (46, 50, 54) stitches remain. (See step-by-step instructions.) Continue to work in St st until piece measures 17" (18", 19", 21") from cast-on edge, ending with a WS row. Bind off all stitches loosely.

FRONT:
(make 2, reverse shaping)

With #9 needle and **color A,** cast on 28 (30, 32, 34) stitches. Work in K2, P2 ribbing for 6 rows as follows: For 4–5 and 8–9 sizes: K2, P2 every row. For 6–7 and 10+ sizes: **Row 1 (RS):** K2, *P2, K2* to end. **Row 2:** P2, *K2, P2* to end. Repeat rows 1 and 2 twice more. Change to #10½ needles and work in St st until piece measures 10" (10½", 11", 12½") from cast-on edge, ending with a WS row for the left front and a RS row for the right front. SHAPE ARMHOLES AS FOR BACK AT OUTSIDE EDGE ONLY until 21 (23, 25, 27) stitches remain. (See step-by-step instructions.) Continue to work in St st until piece measures 14½" (15½", 16½", 18½") from cast-on edge, ending with a RS row for the left front and a WS row for the right front. SHAPE CREW NECK: At beginning of neck edge, every other row, bind off 4 stitches once, 3 stitches once, 2 stitches once, 1 stitch 1 (1, 2, 2) times. (See step-by-step

instructions.) Continue to work in St st on remaining 11 (13, 14, 16) stitches until piece measures 17" (18", 19", 21") from cast-on edge, ending with a WS row. Bind off all stitches loosely.

SLEEVES:

With #9 needle and **color A,** cast on 26 (28, 30, 32) stitches. Work in K2, P2 ribbing for 6 rows as follows: For 6–7 and 10+ sizes: K2, P2 every row. For 4–5 and 8–9 sizes: **Row 1 (RS):** K2, *P2, K2* to end. **Row 2:** P2, *K2, P2* to end. Repeat rows 1 and 2 twice more. Change to 10½ needle and work in St st. **AT THE SAME TIME,** increase 1 stitch at each edge, every 6th row 5 times and then every 4th row 3 (4, 5, 6) times until you have 42 (46, 50, 54) stitches.

Note: Increase leaving 2 edge stitches on either side of work. This means you should knit 2 stitches, increase 1 stitch, knit to the last 2 stitches, increase 1 stitch, and then knit the remaining 2 stitches. Increasing like this makes it easier to sew up your seams.

When sleeve measures 11½" (12½", 14", 15") from cast-on edge, end with a WS row. SHAPE CAP: Bind off 3 stitches at the beginning of the next 2 rows. Bind off 2 stitches at the beginning of the next 2 rows. Then decrease 1 stitch at each edge, every other row twice. Bind off 2 stitches at the beginning of the next 10 (12, 14, 14) rows until 8 (8, 8, 12) stitches remain. Bind off all stitches loosely.

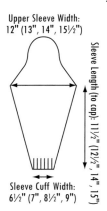

Upper Sleeve Width: 12" (13", 14", 15½")

Sleeve Length (to cap): 11½" (12½", 14", 15")

Sleeve Cuff Width: 6½" (7", 8½", 9")

FINISHING:

Sew shoulder seams together. Sew sleeves on. Sew up side and sleeve seams.

Note: Buttonholes are placed on the right side for girls and the left side for boys.

BUTTON BAND: (This is the right side when made for a boy and left side when made for a girl.) With #9 needle, **color B,** and RS facing, pick up 60 (64, 68, 72) stitches. Work in K2, P2 ribbing for 5 rows. Bind off all stitches loosely.

BUTTONHOLE BAND: (This is the right side when made for a girl and left side when made for a boy.) With #9 needle, **color B,** and RS facing, pick up 60 (64, 68, 72) stitches. **Rows 1 and 2:** K2, P2 ribbing. **Row 3:** Rib 3, *YO, Rib2tog, Rib 11 (12, 13, 14)*. Repeat from * to * 3 more times, end YO, Rib2tog, Rib 3. **Rows 4 and 5:** K2, P2 ribbing. Bind off all stitches loosely.

NECKBAND: With #9 needle, **color C,** and RS facing, pick up 54 (58, 62, 66) stitches around the neck. Work in K2, P2 ribbing for 4½" (4½", 5", 5½") as follows: **Row 1:** K2 (P2, K2). **Row 2:** P2 (K2, P2). Bind off all stitches loosely. Sew on buttons.

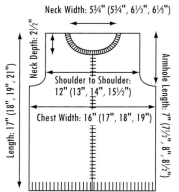

Neck Width: 5¾" (5¾", 6⅓", 6⅓")

Neck Depth: 2½"

Shoulder to Shoulder: 12" (13", 14", 15½")

Chest Width: 16" (17", 18", 19")

Length: 17" (18", 19", 21")

Armhole Length: 7" (7½", 8", 8½")

STEP-BY-STEP GUIDE TO SHAPING THE ARMHOLES

BACK

ROW 1 (RS): Bind off 3 stitches. Knit to end of row.

ROW 2: Bind off 3 stitches. Purl to end of row.

ROW 3: Bind off 2 stitches. Knit to end of row.

ROW 4: Bind off 2 stitches. Purl to end of row.

ROW 5: K2, SSK, knit to last 4 stitches, K2tog, K2.

ROW 6: Purl.

Repeat rows 5 and 6 once more.

LEFT FRONT
(left side when worn)

(You will be binding off on a RS row)

ROW 1 (RS): Bind off 3 stitches. Knit to end of row.

ROW 2: Purl.

ROW 3: Bind off 2 stitches. Knit to end of row.

ROW 4: Purl.

ROW 5: K2, SSK, knit to end of row.

ROW 6: Purl.

Repeat rows 5 and 6 once more.

RIGHT FRONT
(right side when worn)

(You will be binding off on a WS row)

ROW 1 (WS): Bind off 3 stitches. Purl to end of row.

ROW 2: Knit.

ROW 3: Bind off 2 stitches. Purl to end of row.

ROW 4: Knit to last 4 stitches, K2tog, K2.

ROW 5: Purl.

Repeat rows 4 and 5 once more.

LEFT FRONT

(left side when worn)

ROW 1 (WS): Bind off 4 stitches. Purl to end of row.

ROW 2: Knit.

ROW 3: Bind off 3 stitches. Purl to end of row.

ROW 4: Knit.

ROW 5: Bind off 2 stitches. Purl to end of row.

ROW 6: Knit.

ROW 7: Bind off 1 stitch. Purl to end of row.

Repeat rows 7 and 8 0 (0, 1, 1) more time.

RIGHT FRONT

(right side when worn)

ROW 1 (RS): Bind off 4 stitches. Knit to end of row.

ROW 2: Purl.

ROW 3: Bind off 3 stitches. Knit to end of row.

ROW 4: Purl.

ROW 5: Bind off 2 stitches. Knit to end of row.

ROW 6: Purl.

ROW 7: Bind off 1 stitch. Knit to end of row.

ROW 8: Purl.

Repeat rows 7 and 8 0 (0, 1, 1) more time.

* When you are done with the bind-off instructions, compare the length of the front piece to the length of the back. If the front and back measure the same, bind off the remaining stitches loosely. If the front is too short, continue knitting and purling until the pieces are of equal length, then bind off loosely.

supersize me

YARN: Koigu, KPPPM (175 yards / 50g ball)

FIBER CONTENT: 100% merino wool

COLORS:

GIRL VERSION: P803

BOY VERSION: P312

AMOUNT: 9 (10, 11, 12) balls

TOTAL YARDAGE: 1,575 (1,750, 1,925, 2,100) yards

GAUGE: 4½ stitches = 1 inch; 18 stitches = 4 inches

NEEDLE SIZE: US #9 (5.5mm) for body or size needed to obtain gauge; circular 32" US #7 (4.5mm) for ribbings

SIZES: 4–5 (6–7, 8–9, 10+)

KNITTED MEASUREMENTS: Width = 16" (17", 18", 19"), Length = 17" (18", 19", 21"), Sleeve Length = 11½" (12½", 14", 15")

OTHER MATERIALS: 5 buttons

* Yarn is worked double throughout the sweater—this means you should hold 2 strands of yarn together as though they are 1.*

When Deena was pregnant with her third child, she decided to knit the new baby a hooded cardigan with a garter border from *The Yarn Girls' Guide to Kid Knits*. Her oldest daughter, Rena, saw her knitting and automatically thought the sweater was for her. When Deena finished the project, she held it up to show her husband, Alex, and Rena's eyes filled with tears. She said, "I love it, but, Mom, it's too small for me." Deena explained that the pattern book was for babies. She called us the next day and asked us to write the pattern for a bigger size to fit Rena.

BACK:

With #7 needle and 2 strands of yarn, cast on 72 (76, 80, 84) stitches. Work in K2, P2 ribbing for 6 rows as follows: K2, P2 every row. Change to #9 needle and work in St st until piece measures 10" (10½", 11", 12½") from cast-on edge, ending with a WS row. SHAPE ARMHOLES: Bind off 4 stitches at the beginning of the next 2 rows. Bind off 3 stitches at the beginning of the next 2 rows. Bind off 2 stitches at the beginning of the next 2 rows. Then decrease 1 stitch at each edge, every other row, once until 52 (56, 60, 64) stitches remain. (See step-by-step instructions.) Continue to work in St st until piece measures 17" (18", 19", 21") from cast-on edge, ending with a WS row. Bind off all stitches loosely.

FRONT:
(make 2, reverse shaping)

With #7 needle and 2 strands of yarn, cast on 36 (38, 40, 42) stitches. Work in K2, P2 ribbing for 6 rows as follows: For 4–5 and 8–9 sizes: K2, P2 every row. For 6–7 and 10+ sizes: **Row 1 (RS):** K2, *P2, K2* to end. **Row 2:** P2, *K2, P2* to end. Repeat rows 1 and 2 twice more. Change to #9 needle and work in St st until piece measures 10" (10½", 11", 12½") from cast-on edge, ending with a WS row for the left front and a RS row for the right front. SHAPE ARMHOLES AS FOR BACK AT OUTSIDE EDGE ONLY until 26 (28, 30, 32) stitches remain. (See step-by-step instructions.) Continue to work in St st until piece measures 14½" (15½", 16½", 18½") from cast-on edge, ending with a RS row for the left front and a WS row for the right front. SHAPE CREW NECK: At beginning of neck edge, every other row, bind off 5 stitches once, 4 stitches once, 3 stitches once, 1 stitch 1 (1, 2, 3) times. (See step-by-step instructions.) Continue to work on remaining 13 (15, 16, 17) stitches until piece measures 17" (18", 19", 21") from cast-on edge, ending with a WS row. Bind off all stitches loosely.

SLEEVES:

With #7 needle and 2 strands of yarn, cast on 34 (36, 38, 40) stitches. Work in K2, P2 ribbing for 6 rows as follows: For 6–7 and 10+ sizes: K2, P2 every row. For 4–5 and 8–9 sizes: **Row 1 (RS):** K2, *P2, K2* to end. **Row 2:** P2, *K2, P2* to end. Repeat rows 1 and 2 twice more. Change to #9 needle and work in St st. **AT THE SAME TIME,** increase one stitch at each edge every 4th row 11 (12, 13, 15) times until you have 56 (60, 64, 70) stitches.

Note: Increase leaving 2 edge stitches on either side of work. This means you should knit 2 stitches, increase 1 stitch, knit to the last 2 stitches, increase 1 stitch, and then knit the remaining 2 stitches. Increasing like this makes it easier to sew up your seams

When sleeve measures 11½" (12½", 14", 15") from cast-on edge, end with a WS row. S H A P E C A P: Bind off 4 stitches at the beginning of the next 2 rows. Bind off 3 stitches at the beginning of the next 2 rows. Bind off 2 stitches at the beginning of the next 2 rows. Then decrease 1 stitch at each edge, every other row, once. Bind off 2 stitches at the beginning of the next 14 (16, 16, 18) rows until 8 (8, 12, 14) stitches remain. Bind off all stitches loosely.

HOOD:

With #9 needle and 2 strands of yarn, cast on 40 (42, 48, 50) stitches. Work in St st for 21" (22", 23", 25"). Bind off all stitches loosely.

FINISHING:

Sew shoulder seams together. Sew sleeves on. Sew up side and sleeve seams. Fold hood in half and sew down the back side. Sew hood onto sweater starting at the middle of the back neck and ending at the end of the neck shaping. With a 32" #7 needle, 2 strands of yarn, and RS facing you, pick up 70 (76, 82, 90) stitches up the right front, 100 (104, 108, 116) stitches around the hood, and 70 (76, 82, 90) stitches down the left front. You will have 240 (256, 272, 296) stitches. F O R G I R L S: **Rows 1 and 2:** K2, P2 ribbing. **Row 3:** Work 170 (180, 190, 206) stitches in K2, P2 ribbing. Place buttonholes as follows: Rib 2 (3, 2, 2), *YO, Rib2tog, Rib 14 (15, 17, 19)* repeat from * to* 3 more times, Rib2tog, YO, Rib 2 (3, 2, 2). Rows 4 and 5: K2, P2 ribbing. Bind off all stitches loosely. Sew on buttons. F O R B O Y S: **Rows 1 and 2:** K2, P2 ribbing. Row 3: Rib 2 (3, 2, 2), *YO, Rib2tog, Rib 14 (15, 17, 19)*. Repeat * to* 3 more times, Rib2tog, YO, Rib 2 (3, 2, 2). Rib to end. **Rows 4 and 5:** K2, P2 ribbing. Bind off all stitches loosely. Sew on buttons.

BACK

ROW 1 (RS): Bind off 4 stitches. Knit to end of row.

ROW 2: Bind off 4 stitches. Purl to end of row.

ROW 3: Bind off 3 stitches. Knit to end of row.

ROW 4: Bind off 3 stitches. Purl to end of row.

ROW 5: Bind off 2 stitches. Knit to end of row.

ROW 6: Bind off 2 stitches. Knit to end of row.

ROW 7: K2, SSK, knit to last 4 stitches, K2tog, K2.

ROW 8: Purl.

LEFT FRONT
(left side when worn)

(You will be binding off on a RS row)

ROW 1 (RS): Bind off 4 stitches. Knit to end of row.

ROW 2: Purl.

ROW 3: Bind off 3 stitches. Knit to end of row.

ROW 4: Purl.

ROW 5: Bind off 2 stitches. Knit to end of row.

ROW 6: Purl.

ROW 7: K2, SSK, knit to end of row.

ROW 8: Purl.

RIGHT FRONT
(right side when worn)

(You will be binding off on a WS row)

ROW 1 (WS): Bind off 4 stitches. Purl to end of row.

ROW 2: Knit.

ROW 3: Bind off 3 stitches. Purl to end of row.

ROW 4: Purl.

ROW 5: Bind off 2 stitches. Purl to end of row.

ROW 6: Knit to last 4 stitches, K2tog, K2.

ROW 7: Purl.

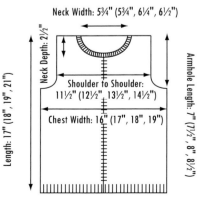

Neck Width: 5¾" (5¾", 6¼", 6½")
Neck Depth: 2½"
Shoulder to Shoulder: 11½" (12½", 13½", 14½")
Chest Width: 16" (17", 18", 19")
Armhole Length: 7" (7½", 8", 8½")
Length: 17" (18", 19", 21")

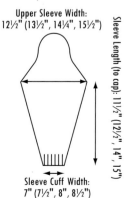

Upper Sleeve Width: 12½" (13½", 14¼", 15½")
Sleeve Length (to cap): 11½" (12½", 14", 15")
Sleeve Cuff Width: 7" (7½", 8", 8½")

STEP-BY-STEP GUIDE TO SHAPING THE CREW NECK

LEFT FRONT

(left side when worn)

ROW 1 (WS): Bind off 5 stitches. Purl to end of row.
ROW 2: Knit.
ROW 3: Bind off 4 stitches. Purl to end of row.
ROW 4: Knit.
ROW 5: Bind off 3 stitches. Purl to end of row.
ROW 6: Knit.
ROW 7: Bind off 1 stitch. Purl to end of row.
ROW 8: Knit.
Repeat rows 7 and 8 0 (0, 1, 2) more times.

RIGHT FRONT

(right side when worn)

ROW 1 (RS): Bind off 5 stitches. Knit to end of row.
ROW 2: Purl.
ROW 3: Bind off 4 stitches. Knit to end of row.
ROW 4: Purl.
ROW 5: Bind off 3 stitches. Knit to end of row.
ROW 6: Purl.
ROW 7: Bind off 1 stitch. Knit to end of row.
ROW 8: Purl.
Repeat rows 7 and 8 0 (0, 1, 2) more times.

* When you are done with the bind-off instructions, compare the length of the front piece to the length of the back. If the front and back measure the same, bind off the remaining stitches loosely. If the front is too short, continue knitting and purling until the pieces are of equal length, then bind off all stitches loosely.

beyond basic cardigans

What do you get if you take a bit of texture then add some color and maybe a few buttons or a zipper? You get beyond basic cardigans. These cardigans incorporate a little something new for you, the knitter. *The Seed Stitch Saga* is knit in seed stitch with a K1, P1 ribbing on the edges and up the button bands. You can think of seed stitch as a messed up rib. Instead of knitting over your knits and purling over your purls you do the very opposite: purl over the knits and knit over the purls. The seed stitch adds a nice texture to the cardigan, especially when using a chunky yarn. *Two Problems, One Solution* is a basic crew neck cardigan that gets a little pizzazz from the many colored stripes in the body of the sweater and the different color used on the ribbings. Lastly, *The Generation Gap* is a great cardigan that has a slightly vintage look. The front panels are worked in a two-color slip stitch pattern and the remainder of the sweater is knit up in a solid color. The slip stitch pattern looks complicated but it really isn't. To slip a stitch you are just moving it from one needle to the other (it's even easier than knitting!). And as you are only working one color at a time, it's as easy as making a striped sweater—it just looks like it required much more talent.

the seed stitch saga

YARN: Manos del Uruguay (136 yards / 100g ball)
FIBER CONTENT: 100% handspun wool
COLORS:
GIRL VERSION: Q
BOY VERSION: U
AMOUNT: 6 (7, 8, 9) balls
TOTAL YARDAGE: 816 (952, 1,088, 1,224) yards
GAUGE: 2$\frac{1}{2}$ stitches = 1 inch; 10 stitches = 4 inches
NEEDLE SIZE: US #13 (9mm) for body or size needed to obtain gauge; US #11 (8mm) for ribbings
SIZES: 4–5 (6–7, 8–9, 10+)
KNITTED MEASUREMENTS: Width = 16" (17", 18", 19"), Length =17" (18", 19", 21"), Sleeve Length = 11$\frac{1}{2}$" (12$\frac{1}{2}$", 14", 15")
OTHER MATERIALS: 5 buttons

* Yarn is worked double throughout the sweater—this means you should hold 2 strands of yarn together as though they are 1. *

Julie's friend Tracy was trying to knit a scarf in seed stitch but she kept getting confused—was she supposed to knit the first stitch or purl it? She just did not understand how this was different than a rib stitch. So Julie explained that seed stitch is just a messed up rib; you knit over your purls and purl over your knits. And if you cast on an odd number of stitches you can K1, P1 every row—you don't have to think about it. Tracy finally got the concept and she finished her scarf. She loved the great texture and the ease of the stitch, so she decided to make this seed stitch cardigan for her son, Ryan.

SEED STITCH:

Over an even number of stitches:
ROW 1: K1, P1.
ROW 2: P1, K1.

Over and even number of stitches:
Every row: K1, P1.

BACK:

With #11 needle and 2 strands of yarn, cast on 40 (42, 46, 48) stitches. Work in K1, P1 ribbing for 6 rows. Change to #13 needle and work in seed stitch until piece measures 10" (10$\frac{1}{2}$", 11", 12$\frac{1}{2}$") from cast-on edge, ending with a WS row. SHAPE ARMHOLES: Bind off 2 stitches at the beginning of the next 2 rows. Then bind off 1 stitch at the beginning of the next 6 rows until 30 (32, 36, 38) stitches remain. (See step-by-step instructions.) Continue to work in seed stitch until piece measures 17" (18", 19", 21") from cast-on edge, ending with a WS row. Bind off all stitches loosely.

FRONT:
(make 2, reverse shaping)

With #11 needle and 2 strands of yarn, cast on 20 (21, 23, 24) stitches. Work in K1, P1 ribbing for 6 rows as follows: For 4–5 and 10+ sizes: K1, P1 every row. For 6–7 and 8–9 sizes: **Row 1:** K1, P1. **Row 2:** P1, K1. Change to #13 needle and work in seed stitch until piece measures 10" (10$\frac{1}{2}$", 11", 12$\frac{1}{2}$") from cast-on edge, ending with a WS row for the left front and a RS row for the right front. SHAPE ARMHOLES AS FOR BACK AT OUTSIDE EDGE ONLY until 15 (16, 18, 19) stitches remain (See step-by-step instructions.) Continue to work in seed stitch until piece measures 14$\frac{1}{2}$" (15$\frac{1}{2}$", 16$\frac{1}{2}$", 18$\frac{1}{2}$") from cast-on edge, ending with a RS row for the left front and a WS row

for the right front. SHAPE CREW NECK: At beginning of neck edge, every other row, bind off 3 stitches once, 2 stitches once, 1 stitch 2 (2, 3, 3) times. (See step-by-step instructions.) Continue to work in seed stitch on remaining 8 (9, 10, 11) stitches until piece measures 17" (18", 19", 21") from cast-on edge, ending with a WS row. Bind off all stitches loosely.

SLEEVES:

With #11 needle and 2 strands of yarn, cast on 18 (20, 22, 24) stitches. Work in K1, P1 ribbing for 6 rows. Change to #13 needle and work in seed stitch. **AT THE SAME TIME,** increase one stitch at each edge every 6th row 6 (6, 7, 7) times until you have 30 (32, 36, 38) stitches.

Note: Increase leaving 2 edge stitches on either side of work. This means you should knit 2 stitches, increase 1 stitch, knit to the last 2 stitches, increase 1 stitch, and then knit the remaining 2 stitches. Increasing like this makes it easier to sew up your seams.

When sleeve measures 11½" (12½", 14", 15") from cast-on edge, end with a WS row. SHAPE CAP: Bind off 2 stitches at the beginning of the next 2 rows. Then bind off 1 stitch at the beginning of the next 6 rows. Bind off 2 stitches at the beginning of the next 6 (6, 8, 8) rows until 8 (10, 10, 12) stitches remain. Bind off all stitches loosely.

FINISHING:

Sew shoulder seams together. Sew sleeves on. Sew up side and sleeve seams.

NECKBAND: With #11 needle, 2 strands of yarn, and RS facing, pick up 36 (36, 40, 40) stitches around the neck. Work in K1, P1 ribbing for 3 (3, 3, 3) rows. Bind off all stitches loosely.

Note: Buttonholes are placed on the right side for girls and the left side for boys.

BUTTON BAND: (This is the right side when made for a boy and left side when made for a girl.) With #11 needle, 2 strands of yarn, and RS facing, pick up 46 (50, 52, 58) stitches. Work in K1, P1 ribbing for 3 rows. Bind off all stitches loosely.

BUTTONHOLE BAND: (This is the right side when made for a girl and left side when made for a boy.) With #11 needle, 2 strands of yarn, and RS facing, pick up 46 (50, 52, 58) stitches. **Row 1:** K1, P1 ribbing. **Row 2:** Rib 2, (2, 3, 2), *YO, Rib2tog, Rib 8 (9, 9, 11)*. Repeat from* to * 3 more times, end YO, Rib2tog, Rib 2 (2, 3, 2). **Row 3:** K1, P1 ribbing. Bind off all stitches loosely. Sew on buttons.

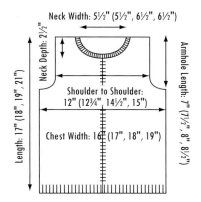

Neck Width: 5½" (5½", 6½", 6½")
Neck Depth: 2½"
Shoulder to Shoulder: 12" (12¾", 14¼", 15")
Chest Width: 16" (17", 18", 19")
Length: 17" (18", 19", 21")
Armhole Length: 7" (7½", 8", 8½")

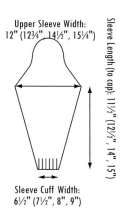

Upper Sleeve Width: 12" (12¾", 14½", 15¼")
Sleeve Length (to cap): 11½" (12½", 14", 15")
Sleeve Cuff Width: 6½" (7½", 8", 9")

STEP-BY-STEP GUIDE TO SHAPING THE ARMHOLES

BACK

ROW 1 (RS): Bind off 2 stitches. Seed stitch to end of row.
ROW 2: Bind off 2 stitches. Seed stitch to end of row.
ROW 3: Bind off 1 stitch. Seed stitch to end of row.
ROW 4: Bind off 1 stitch. Seed stitch to end of row.
Repeat rows 3 and 4 twice more.

LEFT FRONT AND RIGHT FRONT

(You will be binding off on a RS row for left front and a WS row for right front)
ROW 1: Bind off 2 stitches. Seed stitch to end of row.
ROW 2: Seed stitch.
ROW 3: Bind off 1 stitch. Seed stitch to end of row.
ROW 4: Seed stitch.
Repeat rows 3 and 4 twice more.

STEP-BY-STEP GUIDE TO SHAPING THE CREW NECK

(You will be binding off on a WS row for left front and a RS row for right front)
ROW 1 (WS): Bind off 3 stitches. Seed stitch to end of row.
ROW 2: Seed stitch.
ROW 3: Bind off 2 stitches. Seed stitch to end of row.
ROW 4: Seed stitch.
ROW 5: Bind off 1 stitch. Seed stitch to end of row.
ROW 6: Seed stitch.
Repeat rows 5 and 6 1 (1, 2, 2) more times.

* When you are done with the decrease instructions, compare the length of the front to the length of the back. If the front and back measure the same, bind off the remaining stitches loosely. If the front is too short, continue knitting and purling until the pieces are of equal length, then bind off all stitches loosely.

two problems, one solution

YARN: Manos del Uruguay, Cotton Stria (116 yards / 50g ball)
FIBER CONTENT: 100% pure peruvian cotton kettle dyed
COLORS:
GIRL VERSION: A-205, B-204, C-206, D-211
BOY VERSION: A-216, B-203, C-215, D-211
AMOUNT: 1 (1, 2, 2) ball(s) color A; 3 (3, 4, 4) balls color B; 2 (3, 3, 4) balls color C; 2 (3, 3, 4) balls color D
TOTAL YARDAGE: 116 (116, 232, 232) yards color A; 348 (348, 464, 464) yards color B; 232 (348, 348, 464) yards color C; 232 (348, 348, 464) yards color D
GAUGE: $3\frac{1}{4}$ stitches = 1 inch; 13 stitches = 4 inches
NEEDLE SIZE: US #$10\frac{1}{2}$ (6.5mm) for body or size needed to obtain gauge; US #9 (5.5mm) for neck and button band ribbing
SIZES: 4–5 (6–7, 8–9, 10+)
KNITTED MEASUREMENTS: Width = 16" (17", 18", 19"), Length =17" (18", 19", 21"), Sleeve Length = $11\frac{1}{2}$" ($12\frac{1}{2}$", 14", 15")
OTHER MATERIALS: 5 buttons

* Yarn is worked double throughout the sweater—this means you should hold 2 strands of yarn together as though they are 1.*

When Patricia was pregnant, Jake, her three-year-old son, got upset when she left him with the babysitter so she could go to her obstetrician. Patricia's doctor always ran late, and Patricia wanted something she could do while she waited. She decided that knitting a sweater for Jake would solve two problems at once. First, she could keep herself busy while she waited to see her doctor. Second, she thought it would make her trips to the doctor easier on Jake if he knew she was knitting him a surprise while she was there. She came in, and we helped her choose some great colors of soft cotton to knit in stripes. When Jake went to visit Patricia at the hospital after she had given birth to his new sister, she gave him the new sweater as a gift from mom and baby.

STRIPED ST ST:

2 rows color B

4 rows color C

4 rows color D

BACK:

With #9 needle and 2 strands of **color A,** cast on 52 (56, 60, 64) stitches. Work in K2, P2 ribbing for 6 rows as follows: K2, P2 every row. Change to #$10\frac{1}{2}$ needle and work in Striped St st until piece measures 10" ($10\frac{1}{2}$", 11", $12\frac{1}{2}$") from cast-on edge, ending with a WS row.

SHAPE ARMHOLES: Bind off 3 stitches at the beginning of the next 2 rows. Bind off 2 stitches at the beginning of the next 2 rows. Then decrease 1 stitch at each edge, every other row twice until 38 (42, 46, 50) stitches remain. (See step-by-step instructions.) Continue to work in Striped St st until piece measures 17" (18", 19", 21") from

cast-on edge, ending with a WS row. Bind off all stitches loosely.

FRONT:
(make 2, reverse shaping)

With #9 needle and 2 strands of color A, cast on 26 (28, 30, 32) stitches. Work in K2, P2 ribbing for 6 rows as follows: For 6–7 and 10+ sizes: K2, P2 every row. For 4–5 and 8–9 sizes: **Row 1 (RS):** K2, *P2, K2* to end. **Row 2:** P2, *K2, P2* to end. Change to #10½ needle and work in Striped St st until piece measures 10" (10½", 11", 12½") from cast-on edge, ending with a WS row for the left front and a RS row for the right front. SHAPE ARMHOLES AS FOR BACK AT OUTSIDE EDGE ONLY until 19 (21, 23, 25) stitches remain. (See step-by-step instructions.) Continue to work in Striped St st until piece measures 14½" (15½", 16½", 18½") from cast-on edge, ending with a RS row for the left front and a WS row for the right front. SHAPE CREW NECK: At beginning of neck edge, every other row, bind off 4 stitches once, 3 stitches once, 2 stitches once, 1 stitch 1 (1, 2, 2) times. (See step-by-step instructions.) Continue to work in striped St st on remaining 9 (11, 12, 14) stitches until piece measures 17" (18", 19", 21") from cast-on edge, ending with a WS row. Bind off all stitches loosely.

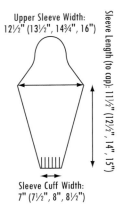

Upper Sleeve Width: 12½" (13½", 14¾", 16")

Sleeve Length (to cap): 11½" (12½", 14", 15")

Sleeve Cuff Width: 7" (7½", 8", 8½")

SLEEVES:

With #9 needle and 2 strands of **color A,** cast on 24 (26, 28, 30) stitches. Work in K2, P2 ribbing for 6 rows as follows: For 4–5 and 8–9 sizes: K2, P2 every row. For 6–7 and 10+ sizes: **Row 1 (RS):** K2, *P2, K2* to end. **Row 2:** P2, *K2, P2* to end. Repeat rows 1 and 2 twice more. Change to #10½ needle and work in Striped St st. **AT THE SAME TIME,** increase one stitch at each edge every 6th row 5 times and then every 4th row 3 (4, 5, 6) times until you have 40 (44, 48, 52) stitches.

Note: Increase leaving 2 edge stitches on either side of work. This means you should knit 2 stitches, increase 1 stitch, knit to the last 2 stitches, increase 1 stitch, and then knit the remaining 2 stitches. Increasing like this makes it easier to sew up your seams.

When sleeve measures 11½" (12½", 14", 15") from cast-on edge, end with a WS row. SHAPE CAP: Bind off 3 stitches at the beginning of the next 2 rows. Bind off 2 stitches at the beginning of the next 2 rows. Then decrease 1 stitch at each edge, every other row twice. Bind off 2 stitches at the beginning of the next 10 (12, 12, 14) rows until 6 (6, 10, 10) stitches remain. Bind off all stitches loosely.

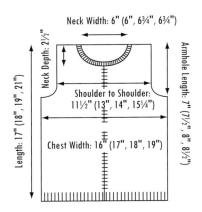

Neck Width: 6" (6", 6¾", 6¾")

Neck Depth: 2½"

Shoulder to Shoulder: 11½" (13", 14", 15¼")

Chest Width: 16" (17", 18", 19")

Length: 17" (18", 19", 21")

Armhole Length: 7" (7½", 8", 8½")

FINISHING:

Sew shoulder seams together. Sew sleeves on. Sew up side and sleeve seams.

NECKBAND: With #9 needle, 2 strands of **color A,** and RS facing, pick up 52 (52, 56, 56) stitches around neck. Work in K2, P2 ribbing for 5 rows. Bind off all stitches loosely.

Note: Buttonholes are placed on the right side for girls and the left side for boys.

BUTTON BAND: (This is the right side when made for a boy, and left side when made for a girl.) With #9 needle, 2 strands of **color A,** and RS facing, pick up 56 (60, 64, 70) stitches. Work in K2, P2 ribbing for 5 rows. Bind off all stitches loosely.

BUTTONHOLE BAND: (This is the right side when made for a girl, and left side when made for a boy.) With #9 needle, **color A,** and RS facing, pick up 56 (60, 64, 70) stitches. **Rows 1 and 2:** K2, P2 ribbing. **Row 3:** Rib 3 (3, 3, 2), *YO, Rib2tog, Rib 10 (11, 12, 14)*. Repeat from * to * 3 more times, end YO, Rib2tog, Rib 3 (3, 3, 2). **Rows 4 and 5:** K2, P2 ribbing. Bind off all stitches loosely. Sew on buttons.

STEP-BY-STEP GUIDE TO SHAPING THE ARMHOLES

BACK

ROW 1 (RS): Bind off 3 stitches. Knit to end of row.
ROW 2: Bind off 3 stitches. Purl to end of row.
ROW 3: Bind off 2 stitches. Knit to end of row.
ROW 4: Bind off 2 stitches. Purl to end of row.
ROW 5: K2, SSK, knit to last 4 stitches, K2tog, K2.
ROW 6: Purl.
Repeat rows 5 and 6 once more.

LEFT FRONT

(left side when worn)

(You will be binding off on a RS row)
ROW 1 (RS): Bind off 3 stitches. Knit to end of row.
ROW 2: Purl.
ROW 3: Bind off 2 stitches. Knit to end of row.
ROW 4: Purl.
ROW 5: K2, SSK, knit to end of row.
ROW 6: Purl.
Repeat rows 5 and 6 once more.

RIGHT FRONT

(right side when worn)

(You will be binding off on a WS row)
ROW 1 (WS): Bind off 3 stitches. Purl to end of row.
ROW 2: Knit.
ROW 3: Bind off 2 stitches. Purl to end of row.
ROW 4: Knit to last 4 stitches, K2tog, K2.
ROW 5: Purl.
Repeat rows 4 and 5 once more.

STEP-BY-STEP GUIDE TO SHAPING THE CREW NECK

LEFT FRONT

(left side when worn)

ROW 1 (WS): Bind off 4 stitches. Purl to end of row.
ROW 2: Knit.
ROW 3: Bind off 3 stitches. Purl to end of row.
ROW 4: Knit.
ROW 5: Bind off 2 stitches. Purl to end of row.
ROW 6: Knit.
ROW 7: Bind off 1 stitch. Purl to end of row.
ROW 8: Knit.
Repeat rows 7 and 8 0 (0, 1, 1) more time.

RIGHT FRONT

(right side when worn)

ROW 1 (RS): Bind off 4 stitches. Knit to end of row.
ROW 2: Purl.
ROW 3: Bind off 3 stitches. Knit to end of row.
ROW 4: Purl.
ROW 5: Bind off 2 stitches. Knit to end of row.
ROW 6: Purl.
ROW 7: Bind off 1 stitch. Knit to end of row.
ROW 8: Purl.
Repeat rows 7 and 8 0 (0, 1, 1) more time.

* When you are done with the bind-off instructions, compare the length of the front piece to the length of the back. If the front and back measure the same, bind off the remaining stitches loosely. If the front is too short, continue knitting and purling until the pieces are of equal length, then bind off all stitches loosely.

the generation gap

YARN: Blue Sky Alpacas, 100% Alpaca
(110 yards / 50g ball)
FIBER CONTENT: 100% alpaca
COLORS:
GIRL VERSION: A-307, B-46
BOY VERSION: A-403, B-211
AMOUNT: 8 (9, 11, 12) balls color A; 2
(3, 3, 4) balls color B
TOTAL YARDAGE: 880 (990, 1,210, 1,320)
yards color A; 220 (330, 330, 440) yards
color B
GAUGE: 3¾ stitches = 1 inch; 15 stitches
= 4 inches
NEEDLE SIZE: US #9 (5.5mm) for body
or size needed to obtain gauge; US #7
(4.5mm) for ribbing
SIZES: 4–5 (6–7, 8–9, 10+)
KNITTED MEASUREMENTS: Width = 16"
(17", 18", 19"); Length =17" (18", 19", 21");
Sleeve Length = 11.5" (12.5", 14", 15")
OTHER MATERIALS: 5 buttons

* Yarn is worked double throughout the
sweater—this means you should hold
2 strands of A or B together as though
they are 1.*

Judy was cleaning out her attic with her grandson, Luke, when she came across an old sweater that her father used to wear a long time ago. Luke fell in love with the sweater. It had subtle texture and two colors on the front and a solid color on the back and sleeves. Its retro look had definitely come back into style. The problem was that moths had gotten to it and darning could not repair it. Judy decided to bring it to our store to see if we could replicate it. We searched through a few stitch books and found a simple slip stitch pattern using two colors that fit the bill. We wrote her this pattern and Luke loved the sweater. Who knows who will come across this one in the next few generations?

BACK:

With #7 needle and 2 strands of **color A,** cast on 60 (64, 68, 72) stitches. Work in K2, P2 ribbing for 6 rows as follows: K2, P2 every row. Change to #9 needle and work in St st until piece measures 10" (10½", 11", 12½") from cast-on edge, ending with a WS row. SHAPE ARMHOLES: Bind off 3 stitches at the beginning of the next 2 rows. Bind off 2 stitches at the beginning of the next 2 rows. Then decrease 1 stitch at each edge, every other row 3 times until 44 (48, 52, 56) stitches remain. (See step-by-step instructions.) Continue to work in St st until piece measures 17" (18", 19", 21") from cast-on edge, ending with a WS row. Bind off all stitches loosely.

FRONT:
(make 2, reverse shaping)

With #7 needle, and 2 strands of **color A,** cast on 30 (32, 34, 36) stitches. Work in K2, P2 ribbing for 6 rows as follows: For 6–7 and 10+ sizes: K2, P2 every row. For 4–5 and 8–9 sizes: **Row 1 (RS):** K2, *P2, K2* to end. **Row 2:** P2, *K2, P2* to end. Repeat rows 1 and 2 2 more times. Increase 1 stitch at the end of the last row of ribbing. You will now have 31 (33, 35, 37) stitches. Change to #9 nee-dle and work in pattern as follows: **Row 1 (RS):** With **color A,** K1, *bring yarn to front, slip 1 purl-wise, bring yarn to back, K1*. Repeat from * to * to end. **Row 2:** With **color A,** purl. **Row 3:** With **color B,** K1, *K1, bring yarn to front, slip 1 purl-wise, bring yarn to back*. Repeat from * to * until 2 stitches remain, K2. **Row 4:** With **color B,** purl. Repeat the 4 row pattern until piece measures 10" (10½", 11", 12½") from cast-on edge, ending with a WS row for the left front and a RS row for the right front. SHAPE ARMHOLES AS FOR BACK AT OUTSIDE EDGE ONLY until 23 (25, 27, 29) stitches remain. (See step-by-step instructions.)

Continue to work in pattern stitch until piece measures 14½" (15½", 16½", 18½") from cast-on edge, ending with a RS row for the left front and a WS row for the right front. SHAPE CREW NECK: At beginning of neck edge, every other row, bind off 5 stitches once, bind off 3 stitches once, 2 stitches once, 1 stitch 1 (1, 2, 2) times. (See step-by-step instructions.) Continue to work in pattern stitch on remaining 12 (14, 15, 17) stitches until piece measures 17" (18", 19", 21") from cast-on edge, ending with a WS row. Bind off all stitches loosely.

SLEEVES:

With #7 needle and 2 strands of **color A,** cast on 30 (32, 34, 34) stitches. Work in K2, P2 ribbing for 6 rows as follows: For 6–7 size: K2, P2 every row. For 4–5, 8–9, and 10+ sizes: **Row 1 (RS):** K2, *P2, K2* to end. **Row 2:** P2, *K2, P2* to end. Repeat rows 1 and 2 twice more. Change to #9 needle and work in St st. **AT THE SAME TIME,** increase 1 stitch at each edge, every 6th row 7 (8, 9, 11) times until you have 44 (48, 52, 56) stitches.

Note: Increase leaving 2 edge stitches on either side of work. This means you should knit 2 stitches, increase 1 stitch, knit to the last 2 stitches, increase 1 stitch, and then knit the remaining 2 stitches. Increasing like this makes it easier to sew up your seams.

When sleeve measures 11½" (12½", 14", 15") from cast-on edge, end with a WS row. SHAPE CAP: Bind off 3 stitches at the beginning of the next 2 rows. Bind off 2 stitches at the beginning of the next 2 rows. Then decrease 1 stitch at each edge, every other row, 3 times. Bind off 2 stitches at the beginning of the next 8 (10, 10, 12) rows until 12 (12, 16, 16) stitches remain. Bind off all stitches loosely.

FINISHING:

Sew shoulder seams together. Sew sleeves on. Sew up side and sleeve seams.

NECKBAND: With #7 needle, 2 strands of **color A,** and RS facing, pick up 52 (52, 56, 56) stitches around the neck. Work in K2, P2 ribbing for 5 rows. Bind off all stitches loosely.

Note: Buttonholes are placed on the right side for girls and the left side for boys.

BUTTON BAND: (This is the right side when made for a boy and left side when made for a girl.) With #7 needle, 2 strands of **color A,** and RS facing, pick up 76 (80, 84, 96) stitches. Work in K2, P2 ribbing for 5 rows. Bind off all stitches loosely.

BUTTONHOLE BAND: (This is the right side when made for a girl and left side when made for a boy.) With #7 needle, 2 strands of **color A,** and RS facing, pick up 76 (80, 84, 96) stitches. **Rows 1 and 2:** K2, P2 ribbing. **Row 3:** Rib 3, *YO, Rib2tog, Rib 15 (16, 17, 20)*. Repeat from * to * 3 more times, end YO, Rib2tog, Rib 3. **Rows 4 and 5:** K2, P2 ribbing. Bind off all stitches loosely. Sew on buttons.

STEP-BY-STEP GUIDE TO SHAPING THE ARMHOLES

BACK

ROW 1 (RS): Bind off 3 stitches. Knit to end of row.

ROW 2: Bind off 3 stitches. Purl to end of row.

ROW 3: Bind off 2 stitches. Knit to end of row.

ROW 4: Bind off 2 stitches. Purl to end of row.

ROW 5: K2, SSK, knit to last 4 stitches, K2tog, K2.

ROW 6: Purl.

Repeat rows 5 and 6 twice more.

LEFT FRONT
(left side when worn)

(You will be binding off on a RS row)

ROW 1 (RS): Bind off 3 stitches. Pattern stitch to end of row.

ROW 2: Purl.

ROW 3: Bind off 2 stitches. Pattern stitch to end of row.

ROW 4: Purl.

ROW 5: K2tog. Pattern stitch to end of row.

ROW 6: Purl.

Repeat rows 5 and 6 twice more.

RIGHT FRONT
(right side when worn)

(You will be binding off on a WS row)

ROW 1 (WS): Bind off 3 stitches. Purl to end of row.

ROW 2: Pattern stitch.

ROW 3: Bind off 2 stitches. Purl to end of row.

ROW 4: Pattern stitch to last 2 stitches, K2tog.

ROW 5: Purl.

Repeat rows 4 and 5 twice more.

STEP-BY-STEP GUIDE TO SHAPING THE CREW NECK

LEFT FRONT
(left side when worn)

ROW 1 (WS): Bind off 5 stitches. Purl to end of row.

ROW 2: Pattern stitch.

ROW 3: Bind off 3 stitches. Purl to end of row.

ROW 4: Pattern stitch.

ROW 5: Bind off 2 stitches. Purl to end of row.

ROW 6: Pattern stitch.

ROW 7: Bind off 1 stitch. Purl to end of row.

ROW 8: Pattern stitch.

Repeat rows 7 and 8 0 (0, 1, 1) more time.

RIGHT FRONT
(right side when worn)

ROW 1 (RS): Bind off 5 stitches. Pattern stitch to end of row.

ROW 2: Purl.

ROW 3: Bind off 3 stitches. Pattern stitch to end of row.

ROW 4: Purl.

ROW 5: Bind off 2 stitches. Pattern stitch to end of row.

ROW 6: Purl.

ROW 7: Bind off 1 stitch. Pattern stitch to end of row.

ROW 8: Purl.

Repeat rows 7 and 8 0 (0, 1, 1) more time.

* When you are done with the decrease instructions, compare the length of the front piece to the length of the back. If the front and back measure the same, bind off the remaining stitches loosely. If the front is too short, continue working in pattern until the pieces are of equal length, then bind off all stitches.

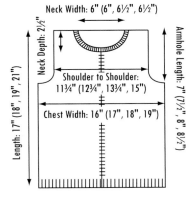

Neck Width: 6" (6", 6½", 6½")

Neck Depth: 2½"

Shoulder to Shoulder: 11¾" (12¾", 13¾", 15")

Armhole Length: 7" (7½", 8", 8½")

Length: 17" (18", 19", 21")

Chest Width: 16" (17", 18", 19")

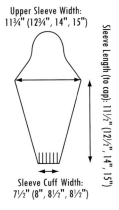

Upper Sleeve Width: 11¾" (12¾", 14", 15")

Sleeve Length (to cap): 11½" (12½", 14", 15")

Sleeve Cuff Width: 7½" (8", 8½", 8½")

T r-necks

It used to be that V-neck sweaters were considered preppy, maybe even a little stodgy. The idea of a V-neck sweater may remind you of a grandfather smoking his pipe. Today, however, V-necks are hip, stylish, and easy to wear—a white T-shirt looks great under almost any V-neck—for boys and girls alike.

There are four V-neck sweaters in this chapter: two pullovers and two cardigans. *Mothers Are Always Right* is a simple rolled-edge pullover. The finishing of the V-neck is incorporated into the neck decreases, leaving the neck edge with a raw, but neat edge. This sweater has a loose, comfy look that kids today are sure to like. *Marissa: An Experienced New Yorker* is a basic V-neck cardigan. This one may look a little like your grandfather's sweater, but who cares—it's a classic look. It'll keep any kid warm, and if you knit it in a cool color or tempting texture, it becomes unique. *The Family That Knits Together Sticks Together* is a super V-neck hoodie. It is knit in one color but has a pocket and a drawstring for the hood that are knit in a contrasting color. This is a great sweater for you to have some fun with color. Use a funky or out of the ordinary hue for the pocket and drawstring to add a little zing. *World Series Winner* is a raglan baseball cardigan. The ribbings and sleeves are knit in one color and the body of the front and back in another. The two-tone sweater with the zipper has a modish, hipster look. And if you want to go for school spirit, you can make it in the kids' school colors, or try making it in their favorite sports team's colors.

mothers are always right

YARN: Zitron, Loft (108 yards / 50g ball)
FIBER CONTENT: 100% new wool
COLORS:
GIRL VERSION: 540
BOY VERSION: 580
AMOUNT: 5 (5, 6, 7) balls
TOTAL YARDAGE: 540 (540, 648, 756) yards
GAUGE: 4 stitches = 1 inch; 16 stitches = 4 inches
NEEDLE SIZE: US #10 (6mm) or size needed to obtain gauge
SIZES: 4–5 (6–7, 8–9, 10+)
KNITTED MEASUREMENTS: Width = 16" (17", 18", 19"), Length = 17" (18", 19", 21"), Sleeve Length = 11½" (12½", 14", 15")

* This sweater has rolled edges. The length of the knitted measurement allows for a 1/2" loss of length due to the rolled edges. *

Sarah, a junior in high school, was under a great deal of stress with college entrance exams, extracurricular activities, and all that homework. Sarah and her mom, Petra, have a very close relationship and Sarah often confides in her mom. In tears one evening, Sarah told her mom that she was having trouble relaxing. Petra knew just the thing—she taught Sarah how to knit. After knitting a scarf, Sarah was ready for a simple sweater. So she came to us and found a fun multicolor yarn that was quick to knit but not too bulky, which would allow her to wear the sweater inside and show off her craftiness in school. The V-neck she chose to knit has simple decreases for the neck, and there's no need to pick up stitches for finishing. Although she was strapped for time, whenever Sarah started to feel stressed she would put down her homework and knit for fifteen minutes. She loved the rhythmic clicking of the needles, and it really did relax her so she could concentrate better on her studies. See? Mothers are always right.

BACK:

With #10 needle, cast on 64 (68, 72, 76) stitches. Work in St st until piece measures 10½" (11", 11½", 13") from cast-on edge, ending with a WS row. SHAPE ARMHOLES: Bind off 3 stitches at the beginning of the next 2 rows. Bind off 2 stitches at the beginning of the next 2 rows. Then decrease 1 stitch at each edge, every other row 3 times until 48 (52, 56, 60) stitches remain. (See step-by-step instructions.) Continue working in St st until piece measures 17½" (18½", 19½", 21½") from cast-on edge, ending with a WS row. Bind off all stitches loosely.

FRONT:

Note: You may be shaping the armhole and the V-neck at the same time. Please read the instructions before proceeding.

Work as for Back until piece measures 10½" (11", 11½", 13") from cast-on edge, ending with a WS row. SHAPE ARMHOLES: Bind off 3 stitches at the beginning of the next 2 rows. Bind off 2 stitches at the beginning of the next 2 rows. Then decrease 1 stitch at each edge, every other row 3 times until 48 (52, 56, 60) stitches remain. (See

step-by-step instructions.) **AT THE SAME TIME,** when piece measures 11½" (12", 12½", 14½") from cast-on edge, ending with a WS row, SHAPE V-NECK: Place a marker at the center. **Row 1 (RS):** Knit until 4 stitches before the marker, K2tog, K2. Turn work around as though you were at the end of the row. You are going to ignore the rest of the stitches. **Row 2:** Purl. **Row 3:** Knit. **Row 4:** Purl.

Repeat rows 1–4 5 more times until 18 (20, 22, 24) stitches remain. Then repeat rows 1 and 2 6 (7, 7, 8) times until 12 (13, 15, 16) stitches remain. Continue to work on remaining stitches until piece measures 17½" (18½", 19½", 21½") from cast-on edge, ending with a WS row. (See step-by-step instructions.) Bind off remaining stitches loosely.

Attach yarn to other side. You should be on a RS row. **Row 1 (RS):** K2, SSK, knit until end. **Row 2:** Purl. **Row 3:** Knit. Row 4: Purl. Repeat rows 1–4 5 more times until 18 (20, 22, 24) stitches remain. Then repeat rows 1 and 2 6 (7, 7, 8) more times until 12 (13, 15, 16) stitches remain. (See step-by-step instructions.) Continue to work on remaining stitches until piece measures 17½" (18½", 19½", 21½") from cast-on edge, ending with a WS row. Bind off remaining stitches loosely.

SLEEVES:

With #10 needle, cast on 30 (32, 34, 36) stitches. Work in St st. **AT THE SAME TIME,** increase one stitch at each edge every 6th row 9 (10, 11, 12) times until you have 48 (52, 56, 60) stitches.

Note: Increase leaving 2 edge stitches on either side of work. This means you should knit 2 stitches, increase 1 stitch, knit to the last 2 stitches, increase 1 stitch, and then knit the remaining 2 stitches. Increasing like this makes it easier to sew up your seams.

When sleeve measures 12½" (13½", 15", 16") from cast-on edge, end with a WS row. SHAPE CAP: Bind off 3 stitches at the beginning of the next 2 rows. Bind off 2 stitches at the beginning of the next 2 rows. Then decrease 1 stitch at each edge, every other row 3 times. Bind off 2 stitches at the beginning of the next 12 (14, 14, 16) rows until 8 (8, 12, 12) stitches remain. Bind off all stitches loosely.

FINISHING:

Sew shoulder seams together. Sew sleeves on. Sew up side and sleeve seams.

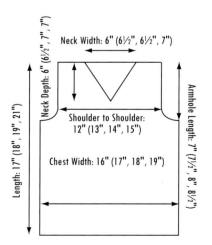

Neck Width: 6" (6½", 6½", 7")

Neck Depth: 6" (6½", 7", 7")

Shoulder to Shoulder: 12" (13", 14", 15")

Armhole Length: 7" (7½", 8", 8½")

Length: 17" (18", 19", 21")

Chest Width: 16" (17", 18", 19")

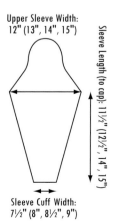

Upper Sleeve Width: 12" (13", 14", 15")

Sleeve Length (to cap): 11½" (12½", 14", 15")

Sleeve Cuff Width: 7½" (8", 8½", 9")

STEP-BY-STEP GUIDE TO SHAPING THE ARMHOLES

Note: Be aware that you might be shaping the armhole and V-neck at the same time. Please read the instructions before proceeding.

ROW 1 (RS): Bind off 3 stitches. Knit to end of row.

ROW 2: Bind off 3 stitches. Purl to end of row.

ROW 3: Bind off 2 stitches. Knit to end of row.

ROW 4: Bind off 2 stitches. Purl to the end of the row.

ROW 5: K2, SSK, knit to last 4 stitches, K2tog, K2.

ROW 6: Purl.

Repeat rows 5 and 6 twice more.

STEP-BY-STEP GUIDE TO SHAPING THE V-NECK

First you must place a marker around the needle in the center of the work.

ROW 1 (RS): Knit to 4 stitches before the marker, K2tog, K2.

ROW 2: Purl.

ROW 3: Knit.

ROW 4: Purl.

Repeat rows 1– 4 5 more times. Then repeat rows 1 and 2 6 (7, 7, 8) times.

Attach yarn to the other side of the V.

ROW 1 (RS): K2, SSK, knit to end of row.

ROW 2: Purl.

ROW 3: Knit.

ROW 4: Purl.

Repeat rows 1– 4 5 more times. Then repeat rows 1 and 2 6 (7, 7, 8) times.

* When you are done with the decrease instructions, compare the length of the front piece to the length of the back. If the front and back measure the same, bind off the remaining stitches loosely. If the front is too short, continue knitting and purling until the pieces are of equal length, then bind off loosely.

marissa: an experienced new yorker

YARN: Classic Elite, Paintbox (110 yards / 100g ball)

FIBER CONTENT: 100% merino wool

COLORS:

GIRL VERSION: 6889

BOY VERSION: 6862

AMOUNT: 4 (5, 6, 7) balls

TOTAL YARDAGE: 440 (550, 660, 770) yards

GAUGE: 3 stitches = 1 inch; 12 stitches = 4 inches

NEEDLE SIZE: US #11 (8mm) for body or size needed to obtain gauge; circular 32" US #9 (5.5mm) for neck and button-band ribbing

SIZES: 4–5 (6–7, 8–9, 10+)

KNITTED MEASUREMENTS: Width = 16" (17", 18", 19"), Length =17" (18", 19", 21"), Sleeve Length = 11½" (12½", 14", 15")

OTHER MATERIALS: 3 buttons

Marissa is a nine-year-old native New Yorker who lives on the Upper West Side of Manhattan. She travels to school on her own, knows how to hail a cab, and is familiar with several subway lines. She enjoys basketball, swimming, acting, singing, drawing, bowling, and scrapbooking. She began knitting about three months ago when her mom's friend showed her how. In this short time, she's made two scarves, a doll blanket, and a poncho. She told us that she wanted her next project to be a cardigan. "But," she warned us, "I like to watch TV, listen to music, and talk to my friends when I knit. So it can't be too hard." We said that was fine. "And," she added, "I only really get to knit about five hours a week. So it can't be something that will take me too long." We said that was also fine. "Anything else we need to know?" we asked. "No," she said. We decided that this simple V-neck cardigan would be perfect for her. It's very easy, it knits on relatively big needles, and best of all, it looks great on.

BACK:

With #9 needle, cast on 48 (52, 54, 58) stitches. Work in K1, P1 ribbing for 6 rows. Change to #11 needle and work in St st until piece measures 10" (10½", 11", 12½") from cast-on edge, ending with a WS row. SHAPE ARMHOLES: Bind off 3 stitches at the beginning of the next 2 rows. Bind off 2 stitches at the beginning of the next 2 rows. Then decrease 1 stitch at each edge, every other row once until 36 (40, 42, 46) stitches remain. (See step-by-step instructions.) Continue to work in St st until piece measures 17" (18", 19", 21") from cast-on edge, ending with a WS row. Bind off all stitches loosely.

FRONT:
(make 2, reverse shaping)

Note: You may be shaping the armhole and the V-neck at the same time. Please read the instructions before proceeding.

With #9 needle, cast on 24 (26, 27, 28) stitches. Work in K1, P1 ribbing for 4 rows as follows: For 4–5, 6–7, and 10+ sizes: K1, P1 every row. For 8–9 size: **Row 1:** K1, P1. **Row 2:** P1, K1. Change to #11 needle and work in St st until piece measures 10" (10½", 11", 12½") from cast-on edge, ending with a WS row for the left front and a RS row for the right front. SHAPE ARMHOLES AS FOR BACK AT OUTSIDE EDGE ONLY until 18 (20, 21, 22) stitches remain. (See step-by-step instructions.) **AT THE SAME TIME** when piece measures 10½" (11", 11½", 13") from cast-on edge, ending with a RS row for the left front and a WS row for the right front, SHAPE V-NECK: For left front when worn: **Row 1 (RS):** Knit until last 4 stitches, K2tog, K2. **Row 2:** Purl. **Row 3:** Knit. **Row 4:** Purl. Repeat rows 1– 4 4 (4, 4, 5) times more until 13 (15, 16, 16) stitches remain. Then repeat rows 1 and 2 3 (5, 5, 4) times until 10 (10, 11, 12) stitches remain.

(See step-by-step instructions.) Continue to work on remaining stitches until piece measures 17" (18", 19", 21") from cast-on edge, ending with a WS row. Bind off all stitches loosely. For right side: **Row 1 (RS):** K2, SSK, knit to end. **Row 2:** Purl. **Row 3:** Knit. **Row 4:** Purl. Repeat rows 1– 4 4 (4, 4, 5) times more until 13 (15, 16, 16) stitches remain. Then repeat rows 1 and 2 3 (5, 5, 4) times until 10 (10, 11, 12) stitches remain. (See step-by-step instructions.) Continue to work on remaining stitches until piece measures 17" (18", 19", 21") from cast-on edge, ending with a WS row. Bind off all stitches loosely.

SLEEVES:

With #9 needle, cast on 22 (24, 26, 26) stitches. Work in K1, P1 ribbing for 6 rows. Change to #11 needle and work in St st. **AT THE SAME TIME,** increase one stitch at each edge every 6th row 7 (7, 8, 9) times until you have 36 (38, 42, 44) stitches.

Note: Increase leaving 2 edge stitches on either side of work. This means you should knit 2 stitches, increase 1 stitch, knit to the last 2 stitches, increase 1 stitch, and then knit the remaining 2 stitches. Increasing like this makes it easier to sew up your seams.

When sleeve measures 11½" (12½", 14", 15") from cast-on edge, end with a WS row. SHAPE CAP: Bind off 3 stitches at the beginning of the next 2 rows. Bind off 2 stitches at the beginning of the next 2 rows. Then decrease 1 stitch at each edge, every other row, once. Bind off 2 stitches at the beginning of the next 8 (8, 10, 10) rows until 8 (10, 10, 12) stitches remain. Bind off all stitches loosely.

FINISHING:

Sew shoulder seams together. Sew sleeves on. Sew up side and sleeve seams. With a circular 32" #9 needle and RS facing, pick up 30 (32, 34, 36)

stitches up the right front to beginning of V-neck shaping, place marker (pm), pick up 20 (21, 22, 23) stitches up right neck, pm, pick up 18 (20, 20, 22) stitches across back neck, pm, pick up 20 (21, 22, 23) down left neck to end of V-neck shaping, pick up 30 (32, 34, 36) stitches down left front. You will have 118 (126, 132, 140) stitches. FOR GIRLS: **Row 1:** K1, P1 ribbing. **Row 2:** Rib 2, *YO, Rib2tog, Rib 10 (11, 12, 13)*. Repeat from* to* once more, Rib2tog, YO, Rib 2. Rib to end. **Rows 3 and 4:** K1, P1 ribbing Bind off all stitches loosely. Sew on buttons. FOR BOYS: **Row 1:** K1, P1 ribbing. **Row 2:** Work 88 (94, 98, 104) stitches in K1, P1 ribbing. Place buttonholes as follows: Rib 2, *YO, Rib2tog, Rib 10 (11, 12, 13)*. Repeat from * to* once more, Rib2tog, YO, Rib 2. **Rows 3 and 4:** K1, P1 ribbing. Bind off all stitches loosely. Sew on buttons.

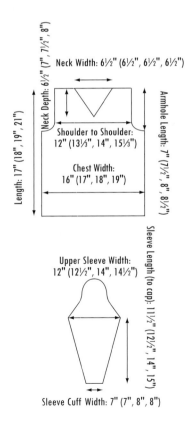

Neck Width: 6½" (6½", 6½", 6½")

Neck Depth: 6½" (7", 7½", 8")

Length: 17" (18", 19", 21")

Armhole Length: 7" (7½", 8", 8½")

Shoulder to Shoulder: 12" (13⅓", 14", 15⅓")

Chest Width: 16" (17", 18", 19")

Upper Sleeve Width: 12" (12½", 14", 14½")

Sleeve Length (to cap): 11½" (12½", 14", 15")

Sleeve Cuff Width: 7" (7", 8", 8")

STEP-BY-STEP GUIDE TO SHAPING THE ARMHOLES

BACK

ROW 1 (RS): Bind off 3 stitches. Knit to end of row.

ROW 2: Bind off 3 stitches. Purl to end of row.

ROW 3: Bind off 2 stitches. Knit to end of row.

ROW 4: Bind off 2 stitches. Purl to end of row.

ROW 5: K2, SSK, knit to last 4 stitches, K2tog, K2.

ROW 6: Purl.

LEFT FRONT

(left side when worn)

(You will be binding off on a RS row)

ROW 1 (RS): Bind off 3 stitches. Knit to end of row.

ROW 2: Purl.

ROW 3: Bind off 2 stitches. Knit to end of row.

ROW 4: Purl.

ROW 5: K2, SSK, knit to end of row.

ROW 6: Purl.

RIGHT FRONT

(right side when worn)

(You will be binding off on a WS row)

ROW 1 (WS): Bind off 3 stitches. Purl to end of row.

ROW 2: Knit.

ROW 3: Bind off 2 stitches. Purl to end of row.

ROW 4: Knit to last 4 stitches, K2tog, K2.

ROW 5: Purl.

STEP-BY-STEP GUIDE TO SHAPING THE V-NECK

LEFT FRONT

(left side when worn)

ROW 1 (RS): Knit to last 4 stitches, K2tog, K2.
ROW 2: Purl
ROW 3: Knit.
ROW 4: Purl.
Repeat rows 1– 4 4 (4, 4, 5) more times. Then repeat rows 1 and 2 3 (5, 5, 4) more times.

RIGHT FRONT

(right side when worn)

ROW 1: K2, SSK, knit to end of row.
ROW 2: Purl.
ROW 3: Knit.
ROW 4: Purl.
Repeat rows 1– 4 4 (4, 4, 5) more times. Then repeat rows 1 and 2 3 (5, 5, 4) more times.

* When you are done with the decrease instructions, compare the length of the front piece to the length of the back. If the front and back measure the same, bind off the remaining stitches loosely. If the front is too short, continue knitting and purling until the pieces are of equal length, then bind off loosely.

the family that knits together, sticks together

YARN: Tahki, Donegal Tweed (184 yards / 100 g ball)
FIBER CONTENT: 100% homespun wool
COLORS:
GIRL VERSION: A-804, B-892
BOY VERSION: A-848, B-869
AMOUNT: 4 (5, 5, 6) balls color A; 1 (1, 1, 1) ball color B
TOTAL YARDAGE: 736 (920, 920, 1,104) yards color A; 184 (184, 184, 184) yards color B
GAUGE: 4½ stitches = 1 inch; 18 stitches = 4 inches
NEEDLE SIZE: US #8 (5mm) or size needed to obtain gauge; circular or 2 double-pointed US #5 (3.75mm) needles for I-cord
SIZES: 4–5 (6–7, 8–9, 10+)
KNITTED MEASUREMENTS: Width = 16" (17", 18", 19"), Length = 17" (18", 19", 21"), Sleeve Length = 11½" (12½", 14", 15")

Angela had eight-year-old twins, a boy and a girl, and they just learned to knit. The three of them came into the store to find a group project. Angela wanted a kid-sized sweater pattern that she could knit with the twins' help. We do not normally advise that knitters share a project because gauges can be different, but we figured the point was really to share this experience. After looking around the shop and through our books, they fell in love with the *Not Your Standard-Issue Sweatshirt* from *The Yarn Girls' Guide to Simple Knits*. We decided to make it more sweatshirty and add a pocket. We realized this is a perfect family project, because the kids can make the hoods, which are just rectangles, and Mom can knit the rest of the sweater.

BACK:

With #8 needle and **color A,** cast on 72 (76, 82, 86) stitches. Work in garter stitch for 6 rows. Continue to work in St st until piece measures 10" (10½", 11", 12½") from cast-on edge, ending with a WS row. SHAPE ARMHOLES:

Bind off 4 stitches at the beginning of the next 2 rows. Bind off 2 stitches at the beginning of the next 2 rows. Then decrease 1 stitch at each edge, every other row twice until 56 (60, 66, 70) stitches remain. (See step-by-step instructions.) Continue working in St st until piece measures 17" (18", 19", 21")

from cast-on edge, ending with a WS row. Bind off all stitches loosely.

Note: You may be shaping the armhole and the V-neck at the same time. Please read the instructions before proceeding.

FRONT:

Work as for Back until piece measures 10" (10½", 11", 12½") from cast-on edge, ending with a WS row. SHAPE ARM-HOLES: Bind off 4 stitches at the beginning of the next 2 rows. Bind off 2 stitches at the beginning of the next 2 rows. Then decrease 1 stitch at each edge, every other row twice until 56 (60, 66, 70) stitches remain. (See step-by-step instructions.) **AT THE SAME TIME** when piece measures 12" (12½", 13", 14½") from cast-on edge, ending with a WS row, SHAPE V-NECK: Place a marker at the center. **Row 1 (RS):** Knit until 7 stitches before the marker, K2tog, K5. Turn work around as though you were at the end of the row. You are going to ignore the rest of the stitches. **Row 2:** K5, purl to end of row. **Row 3:** Knit. **Row 4:** K5, purl to end of row. Repeat rows 1–4 0 (0, 4, 4) times more until 27 (29, 28, 30) stitches remain. Then repeat rows 1 and 2 13 (13, 10, 10) times until 14 (16, 18, 20) stitches remain. Continue to work on these stitches as established until piece measures 17" (18", 19", 21") from cast-on edge, ending with a WS row. (See step-by-step instructions.) Bind off remaining stitches loosely.

Attach yarn to other side. You should be on a RS row. **Row 1 (RS):** K5, SSK, knit to end of row. **Row 2:** Purl until 5 stitches remain, K5. **Row 3:** Knit. **Row 4:** Purl until 5 stitches remain, K5. Repeat rows 1–4 0 (0, 4, 4) times more until 27 (29, 28, 30) stitches remain. Then repeat rows 1 and 2 13 (13, 10, 10) times until 14 (16, 18, 20) stitches remain. (See step-by-step instructions.) Continue to work on these stitches as established until piece

measures 17" (18", 19", 21") from cast-on edge, ending with a WS row. Bind off remaining stitches loosely.

SLEEVES:

With #8 needle and **color A,** cast on 34 (36, 38, 40) stitches. Work in garter stitch for 6 rows. Continue to work in St st. **AT THE SAME TIME,** increase one stitch at each edge every 6th row 10 (11, 13, 14) times until you have 54 (58, 64, 68) stitches.

Note: Increase leaving 2 edge stitches on either side of work. This means you should knit 2 stitches, increase 1 stitch, knit to the last 2 stitches, increase 1 stitch, and then knit the remaining 2 stitches. Increasing like this makes it easier to sew up your seams.

When sleeve measures 11½" (12½", 14", 15") from cast-on edge, end with a WS row. SHAPE CAP: Bind off 4 stitches at the beginning of the next 2 rows. Bind off 2 stitches at the beginning of the next 2 rows. Then decrease 1 stitch at each edge, every other row twice. Bind off 2 stitches at the beginning of the next 10 (12, 14, 16) rows until 18 (18, 20, 20) stitches remain. Bind off all stitches loosely.

HOOD:

With #8 needle and **color A,** cast on 44 (48, 52, 56) stitches. Work as follows: **Row 1 (RS):** Knit. **Row 2:** Purl until 10 stitches remain, K10. Repeat rows 1 and 2 until piece measures 21" (22", 23", 25") from cast- on edge. Bind off loosely.

POCKET:

With #8 needle and **color B,** cast on 41 (43, 45, 47) stitches. Work as follows:
Row 1: Knit.

Row 2: K5, purl to last 5 stitches, K5.
Row 3: K5, SSK, knit until 7 stitches remain, K2tog, K5.
Row 4: As row 2.
Row 5: Knit.
Row 6: As row 2.

Repeat rows 3–6 7 (7, 8, 8) times more until 25 (27, 27, 29) stitches remain. Bind off all stitches loosely.

I-CORD:

Use **color B** to make the I-cord.

Make a 3 stitch I-cord that is 50" long. An I-cord is basically just a knitted tube. You will need 2 double-pointed needles or a circular needle, size 5. To make the I-cord, cast on 3 stitches. Knit each stitch. Slide these stitches back to the other end of the needle. Knit the 3 stitches again—you will be taking the yarn from behind the stitches—this seems weird but it is correct. Slide the stitches to the other end of the needle. Repeat this process until the cord is 50" long. K3tog. Pull yarn through the remaining loop and fasten off.

FINISHING:

Sew shoulder seams together. Sew sleeves on. Sew up side and sleeve seams. Fold the hood in half and sew down the back side (the St st side). Attach the hood to the body of the sweater by sewing it in around the back of the neck and half way down the V.

Fold the garter stitch edge of the hood over the I-cord and sew it down. Make 2 small tassels and attach to each end of the I-cord.

STEP-BY-STEP GUIDE TO SHAPING THE ARMHOLES:

Note: Be aware that you might be shaping the armhole and the V-neck at the same time. Please read the instructions before proceeding.

ROW 1 (RS): Bind off 4 stitches. Knit to end of row.
ROW 2: Bind off 4 stitches. Purl to end of row.
ROW 3: Bind off 2 stitches. Knit to end of row.
ROW 4: Bind off 2 stitches. Purl to end of row.
ROW 5: K2, SSK, knit to last 4 stitches, K2tog, K2.
ROW 6: Purl.
Repeat rows 5 and 6 once more.

STEP-BY-STEP GUIDE TO SHAPING THE V-NECK

First you must place a marker around the needle in the center of the work.

ROW 1 (RS): Knit to 7 stitches before the marker, K2tog, K5.
ROW 2: Knit 5, purl to end of row.
ROW 3: Knit.
ROW 4: Knit 5, purl to end of row.
Repeat rows 1– 4 0 (0, 4, 4) more times. Then repeat rows 1 and 2 13 (13, 10, 10) times.

Attach yarn to the other side of the V.
ROW 1 (RS): K5, SSK, knit to end of row.
ROW 2: Purl until 5 stitches remain, K5.
ROW 3: Knit.
ROW 4: Purl until 5 stitches remain, K5.
Repeat rows 1– 4 0 (0, 4, 4) more times. Then repeat rows 1 and 2 13 (13, 10, 10) times.

* When you are done with the decrease instructions, compare the length of the front piece to the length of the back. If the front and back measure the same, bind off the remaining stitches loosely. If the front is too short, continue knitting and purling until the pieces are of equal length, then bind off loosely.

Upper Sleeve Width: 12" (12¾", 14¼", 15")

Sleeve Length (to cap): 11½" (12½", 14")

Sleeve Cuff Length: 7½" (8", 8½", 8¾")

Neck Depth: 5" (5½", 6", 6½")

Neck Width: 5¾" (5¾", 6½", 6½")

Armhole Length: 7" (7½", 8", 8½")

Length: 17" (18", 19", 21")

Shoulder to Shoulder: 12½" (13⅓", 14½", 15½")

Chest Width: 16" (17", 18", 19")

113

world series winner

YARN: Karabella, Aurora Bulky (56 yards / 50g ball)

FIBER CONTENT: 100% extrafine merino wool

COLORS:

GIRL VERSION: A-26, B-25

BOY VERSION: A-24, B-2

AMOUNT: 5 (6, 7, 8) balls color A; 6 (7, 9, 10) balls color B

TOTAL YARDAGE: 280 (336, 392, 448) yards color A; 336 (392, 504, 560) yards color B

STITCH GAUGE: 3½ stitches = 1 inch; 14 stitches = 4 inches

ROW GAUGE: 5 rows = 1 inch; 20 rows = 4 inches

NEEDLE SIZE: US #10½ (6.5mm) for body or size needed to obtain gauge; circular 32" US #9 (5.5mm) for neck and front band ribbing

SIZES: 4–5 (6–7, 8–9, 10+)

KNITTED MEASUREMENTS: Width = 16" (17", 18", 19"), Length =17" (18", 19", 21"), Sleeve Length = 11½" (12½", 14", 15")

OTHER MATERIALS: 1 zipper

Bill is a huge Red Sox fan. His sons are die-hard Yankee supporters. Needless to say, over the past few seasons there has been a little tension in that household come playoff time. Several years ago, Deb decided to knit all her boys this baseball-inspired cardigan. Its raglan sleeves are knit in one color with the body knit in another. The boys got blue and white ones and Bill got blue and red, and they all wore their sweaters during the games. Like many baseball fanatics, Bill and his sons believe in the occasional superstition or curse, and Bill began to notice a pattern emerging with his sons' sweaters: When Quentin wore his sweater but Teddy didn't, the Sox won. So last year when Bill got playoff tickets to Game Seven—the Yankees versus the Red Sox—on the way out the door to the game, Bill nonchalantly grabbed Quentin's sweater and handed Teddy a fleece ... Now the boys can no longer tease their dad about the Curse of the Bambino.

Note: Armhole decreases on the back and sleeves should be done as follows: k2, ssk, knit until 4 stitches remain, k2tog, k2.

For left front: K2, SSK.

For right front: Knit until last 4 stitches, K2tog, K2.

Neck decrease on the right front: K2, SSK, knit until end of row.

Neck decrease on the left front: Knit until end of row, K2tog, K2.

BACK:

With #9 needle and **color B,** cast on 56 (60, 64, 68) stitches. Work in K1, P1 ribbing for 4 rows. Change to #10½ needle and **color A** and work in St st until piece measures 9" (9 3/4", 10½", 12") from cast-on edge, ending with a WS row. SHAPE RAGLAN ARM-HOLES: Bind off 2 stitches at the beginning of the next 2 rows. Work even for 4 rows. Then decrease 1 stitch at each edge, every 4th row 3 (3, 3, 2) times. Then decrease 1 stitch each edge, every other row 13 (14, 15, 18) times until 20 (22, 24, 24) stitches remain. (See step-by-step instructions.) Bind off all stitches loosely on the next purl row.

LEFT FRONT:

With #9 needle and **color B,** cast on 29 (31, 33, 35) stitches. Work in K1, P1 ribbing for 4 rows as follows: Row 1 (RS): K1, P1. Row 2: P1, K1. Change to #10½ needle and **color A** and work in St st until piece measures 9" (9 3/4", 10½", 12") from cast-on edge, ending with a WS row. SHAPE RAGLAN ARMHOLES:

ROW 1 (RS): Bind off 2 stitches

ROW 2: Purl.

ROW 3: Knit.

ROW 4: Purl.

ROW 5: K2, SSK, knit to end of row.

ROW 6: Purl.

ROW 7: Knit.

ROW 8: Purl.

FOR 4–5 AND 6–7 SIZES ONLY: ROW 9: K2, SSK, knit until 4 stitches remain, K2 tog, K2.

FOR 8–9 AND 10+ SIZES ONLY: ROW 9: K2, SSK, knit to end of row.

ROW 10: Purl.

FOR 4–5, 6–7 AND 8–9 SIZES ONLY: ROW 11: Knit.

FOR 10+ SIZE ONLY: ROW 11: K2, SSK, knit to end of row.

ROW 12: Purl.

FOR 4–5, 6–7 AND 8–9 SIZES ONLY: ROW 13: K2, SSK, knit until 4 stitches remain, K2tog, K2.

FOR 10+ SIZE ONLY: ROW 13: K2, SSK, knit to end of row.

ROW 14: Purl.

FOR 4–5, 6–7 AND 8–9 SIZES ONLY: ROW 15: K2, SSK, knit to end of row.

FOR 10+ SIZE ONLY: ROW 15: K2, SSK, knit until 4 stitches remain, K2tog, K2.

ROW 16: Purl.

FOR 4–5, 6–7 AND 8–9 SIZES ONLY: ROW 17: K2, SSK, knit until 4 stitches remain, K2tog, K2.

FOR 10+ SIZE ONLY: ROW 17: K2, SSK, knit to end of row.

ROW 18: Purl.

Repeat rows 15–18 4 more times (rows 19–34).

FOR 4–5 AND 6–7 SIZES ONLY: ROW 35: K2, SSK, knit to end of row.

FOR 8–9 AND 10+ SIZES ONLY: ROW 35: K2, SSK, knit until 4 stitches remain, K2tog, K2.

ROW 36: Purl.

FOR 4–5 SIZE ONLY: ROW 37: K1, SSK, K2tog, K1.

FOR 6–7, 8–9, AND 10+ SIZES ONLY: ROW 37: K2, SSK, knit until 4 stitches remain, K2tog, K2.

ROW 38: Purl.

FOR 4–5 SIZE ONLY: ROW 39: SSK, K2tog.

FOR 6–7 SIZE ONLY ROW 39: K1, SSK, K2tog, K1.

FOR 8–9 AND 10+ SIZES ONLY: ROW 39: K2, SSK, knit until 4 stitches remain, K 2tog, K2.

FOR 4–5 SIZE ONLY: ROW 40: P2tog. Pull yarn through remaining loop and fasten off.

FOR 6–7, 8–9, AND 10+ SIZES ONLY: ROW 40: Purl.

FOR 6–7 SIZE ONLY: ROW 41: SSK, K2tog.

FOR 8–9 SIZE ONLY: ROW 41: K1, SSK, K2tog, K1.

FOR 10+ SIZE ONLY: ROW 41: K2, SSK, K2tog, K2.

FOR 6–7 SIZE ONLY: ROW 42: P2tog. Pull yarn through remaining loop and fasten off.

FOR 8–9 AND 10+ SIZES ONLY: ROW 42: Purl.

FOR 8–9 SIZE ONLY: ROW 43: SSK, K2tog.

FOR 10+ SIZE ONLY: ROW 43: K1, SSK, K2tog, K1.

FOR 8–9 SIZE ONLY: ROW 44: P2tog. Pull yarn through remaining loop and fasten off.

FOR 10+ SIZE ONLY: ROW 44: Purl.

FOR 10+ SIZE ONLY: ROW 45: SSK, K2tog.

FOR 10+ SIZE: ROW 46: P2tog. Pull yarn through remaining loop and fasten off.

RIGHT FRONT:

With #9 needle and **color B,** cast on 29 (31, 33, 35) stitches. Work in K1, P1 ribbing for 4 rows as follows: **Row 1 (RS):** K1, P1. Row 2: P1, K1. Change to #10½ needle and **color A** and work in St st until piece measures 9" (9 3/4", 10½", 12") from cast-on edge, ending with a RS row. SHAPE RAGLAN ARMHOLES:

ROW 1: Bind off 2 stitches.

ROW 2: Knit.

ROW 3: Purl.

ROW 4: Knit until 4 stitches remain, K2tog, K2.

ROW 5: Purl.

ROW 6: Knit.

ROW 7: Purl.

FOR 4–5 AND 6–7 SIZES ONLY: ROW 8: K2, SSK, knit until 4 stitches remain, K2 tog, K2.

FOR 8–9 AND 10+ SIZES ONLY: ROW 8: Knit until 4 stitches remain K2tog, K2.

ROW 9: Purl.

FOR 4–5, 6–7, AND 8–9 SIZES ONLY: ROW 10: Knit.

FOR 10+ SIZE ONLY: ROW 10: Knit until 4 stitches remain, K2tog, K2.

ROW 11: Purl.

FOR 4–5, 6–7, AND 8–9 SIZES ONLY: ROW 12: K2, SSK, knit until 4 stitches remain, K2tog, K2.

FOR 10+ SIZE ROW 12: Knit until 4 stitches remain, K2tog, K2.

ROW 13: Purl.

FOR 4–5, 6–7, AND 8–9 SIZES ONLY: ROW 14: Knit until 4 stitches remain, K2tog, K2.

FOR 10+ SIZE ONLY: ROW 14: K2, SSK, knit until 4 stitches remain, K2tog, K2.

ROW 15: Purl.

FOR 4–5, 6–7, AND 8–9 SIZES ONLY: ROW 16: K2, SSK, knit until 4 stitches remain, K2tog, K2.

FOR 10+ SIZE ONLY: ROW 16: K2, knit until 4 stitches remain, K2tog, K2.

ROW 17: Purl.

Repeat rows 14–17 4 more times (rows 18–33).

FOR 4–5 AND 6–7 SIZES ONLY: ROW 34: Knit until 4 stitches remain, K2tog, K2.

FOR 8–9 AND 10+ SIZES ONLY: ROW 34:

K2, SSK, knit until 4 stitches remain, K2tog, K2.

ROW 35: Purl.

FOR 4–5 SIZE ONLY: ROW 36: K1, SSK, K2tog, K1.

FOR 6–7, 8–9, AND 10+ SIZES ONLY: ROW 36: K2, SSK, knit until 4 stitches remain, K2tog, K2.

ROW 37: Purl.

FOR 4–5 SIZE ONLY: ROW 38: SSK, K2tog.

FOR 6–7 SIZE ONLY: ROW 38: K1, SSK, K2tog, K1.

FOR 8–9 AND 10+ SIZES ONLY: ROW 38: K2, SSK, knit until 4 stitches remain, K 2tog, K2.

FOR 4–5 SIZE ONLY: ROW 39: P2tog. Pull yarn through remaining loop and fasten off.

FOR 6–7, 8–9, AND 10+ SIZES ONLY: ROW 39: Purl.

FOR 6–7 SIZE ONLY: ROW 40: SSK, K2tog.

FOR 8–9 SIZE ONLY: ROW 40: K1, SSK, K2tog, K1.

FOR 10+ SIZE ONLY: ROW 40: K2, SSK, K2tog, K2.

FOR 6–7 SIZE ONLY: ROW 41: P2tog. Pull yarn through remaining loop and fasten off.

FOR 8–9 AND 10+ SIZES ONLY: ROW 41: Purl.

FOR 8–9 SIZE ONLY: ROW 42: SSK, K2tog.

FOR 10+ SIZE ONLY: ROW 42: K1, SSK, K2tog, K1.

FOR 8–9 SIZE ONLY: ROW 43: P2tog. Pull yarn through remaining loop and fasten off.

FOR 10+ SIZE ONLY: ROW 43: Purl.

FOR 10+ SIZE ONLY: ROW 44: SSK, K2tog.

FOR 10+ SIZE ONLY: ROW 45: P2tog. Pull yarn through remaining loop and fasten off.

SLEEVES:

With #9 needle and **color B,** cast on 26 (28, 30, 32) stitches. Work in K1, P1 ribbing for 6 rows. Change to #10½ needle and work in St st. **AT THE SAME TIME,** increase 1 stitch at each edge, every 6th row 8 (8, 9, 10) times until you have 42 (44, 48, 52) stitches.

Note: Increase leaving 2 edge stitches on either side of work. This means you should knit 2 stitches, increase 1 stitch, knit to the last 2 stitches, increase 1 stitch, and then knit the remaining 2 stitches. Increasing like this makes it easier to sew up your seams.

When sleeve measures 11½" (12½", 14", 15") from cast-on edge, end with a WS row. SHAPE RAGLAN ARM-

HOLES: Bind off 2 stitches at the beginning of the next 2 rows. Work even for 4 rows. Then decrease 1 stitch at each edge, every 4th row 3 (3, 3, 2) times. Then decrease 1 stitch each edge, every other row 13 (14, 15, 18) times until 6 (6, 8, 8) stitches remain. (See step-by-step instructions.) Bind off all stitches loosely on the next purl row.

FINISHING:

Sew raglan seams together. Sew up side and sleeve seams. With a circular 32" #9 needle, **color B,** and RS facing, pick up 44 (46, 48, 52) stitches up the right front to beginning of V-neck shaping, place marker (pm), pick up 22 (24, 28, 32) stitches up right neck, pm, pick up 4 (4, 6, 6) stitches across right sleeve, pm, pick up 18 (18, 22, 22) stitches across back neck, pm, pick up 4 (4, 6, 6) stitches across left sleeve, pm, pick up 22 (24, 28, 32) down left neck to end of V-neck shaping, pick up 44 (46, 48, 52) stitches down left front. You will have 158 (166, 186, 202) stitches. Work in K1, P1 ribbing for 5 rows. Bind off all stitches loosely. Sew in zipper.

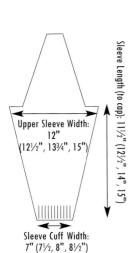

Sleeve Length (to cap): 11½" (12½", 14", 15")

Upper Sleeve Width: 12" (12½", 13¾", 15")

Sleeve Cuff Width: 7" (7½", 8", 8½")

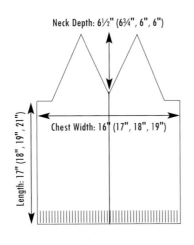

Neck Depth: 6½" (6¾", 6", 6")

Length: 17" (18", 19", 21")

Chest Width: 16" (17", 18", 19")

Armhole Length: 8" (8¼", 8½", 9")

hats

Kids wear hats inside and outside, in cold weather and hot. Hats can be cool, they can be edgy, and they can define a look. Even four-year-olds seem to know this intuitively. The hat makes the kid—and you can make the kid a hat.

The Half-Hour Hat is the simplest rolled-edge hat. It is knit in the round, on large needles. Watch a good half-hour sitcom (or an hour drama if you knit a little more slowly) and bang—you have a hat. *Shock Jock* is a basic hat with a ribbed bottom that turns up, which used to be known as a fisherman's cap. It keeps the ears warm, looks great on, and is a wardrobe staple for the younger set. *All in Due Time* is knit in a 1x1 rib throughout and is striped using two rows of each color. It's got a cool snowboarder look to it but will never go out of style.

half-hour hat

YARN: Alchemy, Lickety Split (60 yards/
100g ball)
FIBER CONTENT: 100% wool
COLORS:
GIRL VERSION: Saffron
BOY VERSION: Tea Leaf
AMOUNT: 1 ball
TOTAL YARDAGE: 60 yards
GAUGE: 2 stitches = 1 inch; 8 stitches =
4 inches
NEEDLE SIZE: circular 16" US #15
(10mm) or size needed to obtain gauge
SIZES: 4–5 (6–7, 8–9, 10+)
KNITTED MEASUREMENTS:
Circumference: 17" (18", 18", 19")

Dana is a new knitter. She'd made several scarves for herself and friends and now wanted to make a hat. "I don't know if I can do it," Dana said nervously. But we assured her that this was a very, very easy hat. All she really had to do was knit, just like with her scarves. We helped Dana cast her stitches onto a circular needle, made sure they weren't twisted, quickly explained the concept of knitting two stitches together, and then sent her on her way. Not more than a half hour later, Dana walked back into the store. We assumed that she'd dropped a stitch or made a mistake of some sort. But instead of asking for help she proudly showed us her finished product.

HAT:

With a 16" #15 needle, cast on 34 (36, 36, 38) stitches. Place a marker at the beginning of your round and join stitches in a circle. Make sure all stitches are facing the same way and that you are not twisting them. Work in St st until piece measures 6" (6½", 6½", 7") from cast-on edge. Begin decreases as follows:

ROUND 1: *K3, K2tog* around.
ROUNDS 2, 4, 6, AND 8: Knit.
ROUND 3: *K2, K2tog* around.
ROUND 5: *K1, K2tog* around.
ROUND 7: *K2tog* around.

FINISHING:

Cut yarn, leaving 10". Thread yarn through remaining loops and pull together; fasten off securely. Weave in ends.

shock jock

YARN: Rowan, Plaid (109 yards / 100 g ball)
FIBER CONTENT: 42% merino wool / 30% acrylic / 28% superfine alpaca
COLORS:
GIRL VERSION: 157
BOY VERSION: 156
AMOUNT: 1 ball
TOTAL YARDAGE: 109 yards
GAUGE: 3 stitches = 1 inch; 12 stitches = 4 inches
NEEDLE SIZE: US #11 (8mm) or size needed to obtain gauge; US #10 (6mm) for ribbing.
SIZES: 4–5 (6–7, 8–9, 10+)
KNITTED MEASUREMENTS:
Circumference: 16" (17", 18", 18½")

Pamela decided to teach a knitting class at her son's all-boy middle school. Thirty-two boys signed up. After a few weeks of classes, Pamela decided the boys were ready to begin a project. She chose this hat pattern with the simple rib at the bottom and stockinette body. Soon after most of the kids had completed their project, Pamela overheard one of the boys—one of the school's jocks—talking to another student. "Knitting is so cool," he said. "Dude, it's like you take this piece of string and in no time it becomes something you can wear . . . look at this awesome hat I made!" Pamela was happily shocked by this boy's enthusiasm and in awe of the craft she was teaching him.

HAT:

With #10 needle, cast on 48 (52, 54, 56) stitches. Work in K2, P2 ribbing for 20 rows as follows: For 4–5, 6–7, and 10+ sizes: K2, P2 every row. For 8–9 size: **Row 1 (RS):** K2, P2. **Row 2:** P2, K2. Change to #11 needle and work in St st until piece measures 7" (7½", 8", 8½") from cast-on edge, ending with a WS row. Begin decreases as follows:

Row 1 (RS): *K4, K2tog* across row.

ROWS 2, 4, 6, AND 8: Purl.

Row 3: *K3, K2tog* across row.

Row 5: *K2, K2tog* across row.

Row 7: *K1, K2tog* across row.

Row 9: *K2tog* across row.

FINISHING:

Cut yarn, leaving 20". Thread yarn through remaining loops and sew down seam. Weave in ends.

all in due time

YARN: Karabella, Aurora Bulky (56 yards / 50g ball)
FIBER CONTENT: 100% extrafine merino wool
COLORS:
GIRL VERSION: A-15, B-25
BOY VERSION: A-21, B-22
AMOUNT: 1 (1, 2, 2) ball(s) color A; 1 (1, 1, 1) ball color B
TOTAL YARDAGE: 56 (56, 112, 112) yards color A; 56 (56, 56, 56) yards color B
GAUGE: 6 stitches = 1 inch; 24 stitches = 4 inches over 1x1 rib
NEEDLE SIZE: US #9 (5.5mm) or size needed to obtain gauge
SIZES: 4–5 (6–7, 8–9, 10+)
KNITTED MEASUREMENTS: Circumference: 12" (13", 13½", 14")

Jordana's husband, Jeff, is a bit spoiled when it comes to sweaters—he prefers cashmere. Well, why not? His wife owns a yarn store. So for the holidays Jordana knit a cashmere hat for him. When Jeff wore it to his family's holiday party, people went wild for it. Jordana got ten requests for the same hat. So she made a list of color preferences and promised they would each get a hat—just not in cashmere.

RIB STRIPE PATTERN:

2 rows K1, P1 in **color B**

2 rows K1, P1 in **color A**

Note: The hat may look small as you are knitting it, but there is a lot of give and it will stretch appropriately when it is worn.

HAT:

With #9 needle and **color A,** cast on 74 (78, 82, 86) stitches. Work in K1, P1 ribbing for 4 rows. Then continue working in rib stripe pattern until piece measures 5" (5 ¼", 5½", 6") from cast-on edge. Begin decreases as follows:

FOR 4–5 SIZE:

ROW 1 (RS): *[K1, P1] twice, K2tog* to last 2 stitches, end K1, P1.
ROW 2: K1, *P2, K1, P1, K1* to last stitch, end P1.
ROW 3: [K1, P1] twice, *K2tog, P1, K1, P1* to last 3 stitches, end K2tog, P1.
ROW 4: *K1, P1.*

ROW 5: K1, P1, K1, *K2tog, P1, K1* to last 3 stitches, end K2tog, P1.
ROW 6: K1, *P2, K1* to last stitch, end K1.
ROW 7: K1, P1, *K2tog, P1.*
ROW 8: *K1, P1.*
ROW 9: K1, *K2tog* to last stitch, K1.

FOR 6–7 SIZE:

ROW 1 (RS): *[K1, P1] twice, K2tog.*
ROW 2: [P1, K1] twice, *P2, K1, P1, K1* to last stitch, end P1.
ROW 3: [K1, P1] twice, *K2tog, P1, K1, P1* to last stitch, end K1.
ROW 4: *P1, K1* to last stitch, end P1.
ROW 5: K1, P1, K1, *K2tog, P1, K1* to last 2 stitches, end K2tog.
ROW 6: *P2, K1* to last 2 stitches, end P1.
ROW 7: K1, P1, *K2tog, P1* to last 2 stitches, end K2tog.
ROW 8: *P1, K1* to last stitch, end P1.
ROW 9: K1, *K2tog.*

FOR 8–9 SIZE:

ROW 1: *[K1, P1] twice, K2tog* to last 4 stitches, end [K1, P1] twice.
ROW 2: *K1, P1, K1, P2* to last 4 stitches, [K1, P1] twice.
ROW 3: [K1, P1] twice, *K2tog, P1, K1, P1.*
ROW 4: *K1, P1.*

ROW 5: K1, P1, K1, *K2tog, P1, K1* to last 3 stitches, end P1, K1, P1.
ROW 6: K1, P1, K1, *P2, K1* to last stitch, end P1.
ROW 7: K1, P1, *K2tog, P1* to last 2 stitches, end K2tog.
ROW 8: *P1, K1* to last stitch, end P1.
ROW 9: K1, *K2tog.*

FOR 10+ SIZE:

ROW 1 (RS): *[K1, P1] twice, K2tog* to last 2 stitches, end K1, P1.
ROW 2: K1, *P2, K1, P1, K1* to last 6 stitches, end P2, [K1, P1] twice.
ROW 3: [K1, P1] 2x, *K2tog, P1, K1, P1* to last 3 stitches, end K2tog, P1.
ROW 4: *K1, P1* to last stitch, end P1.
ROW 5: K1, P1, K1, *K2tog, P1, K1* to last 3 stitches, end K2tog, P1.
ROW 6: *K1, P2* to last 2 stitches, end K1, P1.
ROW 7: K1, P1, *K2tog, P1.*
ROW 8: *K1, P1.*
ROW 9: K1, *K2tog* to last stitch, K1.

FINISHING:

Cut yarn, leaving 20". Thread yarn through remaining loops and sew down seam, lining up stripes up as you go. Weave in ends.

scarves

Scarves are stylin'. Yes, they definitely keep you warm, but they do so much more than that these days. They make statements. They grab attention. They create individuality. Kids these days know who they are or at least who they want to be. And for boys and girls alike, a good scarf can be just the thing to get them there.

Beginner's Luck is knit with super-chunky yarn on a large needle. What makes it different from all the other super-chunky scarves out there is that this one is knit lengthwise, so the stripes are vertical rather than horizontal. To make this scarf, you cast on enough stitches for the length of the scarf and then only have to knit six or seven inches to complete it. It's fun, fast, and a little out of the ordinary. *A Good Scarf Is Hard to Find* is knit in a 3x3 rib. We striped the two colors using four rows of each color and then a third color for the fringe. The combination of colors is fun, and we like to use a color for the fringe that is a bit out of the box. Even though it looks like it might not coordinate, it ends up looking great. We suggest making the fringe pretty long for the girl version but keeping it shorter for the boy version. *Top Ten List* is a classic seed stitch scarf. Go to page 132 to see why you need to make this one.

beginner's luck

YARN: Blue Sky Alpacas, Blue Sky Bulky (45 yards /100g ball)
FIBER CONTENT: 50% alpaca / 50% wool
COLORS:
GIRL VERSION: A-1010, B-1018, C-1014
BOY VERSION: A-1008, B-1012, C-1007
AMOUNT: 1 (1, 2, 2) ball(s) color A; 1 (1, 1, 1) ball color B; 1 (1, 1, 1) ball color C
TOTAL YARDAGE: 45 (45 90, 90) color A; 45 (45, 45, 45) color B; 45 (45, 45, 45) yards color C
GAUGE: 1¾ stitches = 1 inch; 7 stitches = 4 inches
NEEDLE SIZE: Circular 32" US #17 (12mm) or size needed to obtain gauge; large size crochet hook for fringe
SIZES: 4–5 (6–7, 8–9, 10+)
KNITTED MEASUREMENTS: Width = 4" (4", 5", 5"), Length = 45" (50", 52", 55") (not including fringe)

Linda taught herself how to knit from a book and decided to make a scarf with some bulky yarn her friend had given her. She had no idea about patterns or gauge (since then she has read our gauge page and is a master of gauge), so she kept casting on stitches for her scarf and continued to knit and knit. She came into our store and, with an embarrassed look, pulled her knitting out of her bag and said, "I was trying to make a scarf, but it seems a bit too wide and too short, and I am out of yarn." We looked at it and then turned it horizontally. We told her if she bound off, she would actually have a fabulous scarf. This gave us the idea to knit a scarf the same way, but on purpose.

SCARF:

With #17 needle and **color A,** cast on 78 (88, 92, 100) stitches. Work in garter stitch in the following stripe pattern:

FOR 4–5 AND 6–7 SIZES:

2 rows **color A**

2 rows **color B**

2 rows **color C**

2 rows **color B**

2 rows **color A**

Bind off all stitches loosely with **color A.**

FOR 8–9 AND 10+ SIZES:

2 rows **color A**

2 rows **color B**

2 rows **color C**

2 rows **color B**

2 rows **color C**

2 rows **color B**

2 rows **color A**

Bind off all stitches loosely with **color A.**

FINISHING:

With **color A,** cut strands that are approximately 10" long. Put 2 strands together to make each fringe. Using a crochet hook, attach fringe to both ends of the scarf, spacing them as desired.

a good scarf is hard to find

YARN: Filatura di Crosa, Zara (136 yards / 50g ball)
FIBER CONTENT: 100% merino wool
COLORS:
GIRL VERSION: A-1735, B-1717, C-1715
BOY VERSION: A-1503, B-1424, C-1468
AMOUNT: 2 balls color A; 2 balls color B; 1 ball color C
TOTAL YARDAGE: 272 yards color A; 272 yards color B; 136 yards color C
GAUGE: 3½ stitches = 1 inch; 14 stitches = 4 inches
NEEDLE SIZE: US #10 (6mm) or size needed to obtain gauge; medium size crochet hook for fringe
KNITTED MEASUREMENTS: Width = 6", Length = 50"

* Yarn is worked double throughout the scarf—this means you should hold 2 strands of yarn together as though they are 1. *

Allison's son Sam is four years old and he is picky about clothes. From his hat to his shoes, things must match, be comfortable, and be soft. Winter was coming and Allison had recently purchased a new coat for Sam. She also had mittens and a hat that met with his approval, but she was having difficulty finding an acceptable scarf. Fed up with making purchases she had to return, she brought Sam into the store and let him choose the material, colors, and style for his scarf. He looked around for a few minutes, and then came to a quick decision. "I want this soft yarn, in these colors. I think you should stripe these colors and put fringe on the end in this one. And I want the lines that go up and down." Allison agreed and made the scarf to his exact specifications. We liked it so much that we decided to use his pattern for our book.

STRIPE PATTERN:

4 rows in **color A**

4 rows in **color B**

*Note: Do not cut **colors A** and **B** as you stripe. Instead, carry the yarn up one side of the scarf. For example, after you finish 4 rows in **color A**, put down **color A** and pick up **color B**. Begin working with **color B**. For neatest results, after working 2 rows of a color, pick up the color you are not using and simply twist the 2 colors together. Put down the second color and continue the second 2 rows in the color you were using.*

SCARF:

With #10 needle and 2 strands of **color A,** cast on 30 stitches. Work in K3, P3 ribbing in the stripe pattern until piece measures 50" from the cast-on edge, ending with **color A.** Bind off all stitches loosely.

FINISHING:

With **color C,** cut strands of yarn approximately 14" long. Put 6 strands together to make each fringe. Using a crochet hook, attach fringe to both ends of the scarf, placing 1 fringe in each rib.

top ten list

YARN: Jaeger, Baby Merino DK
(131 yards / 50g ball)
FIBER CONTENT: 100% merino wool
COLORS:
GIRL VERSION: 194
BOY VERSION: 191
AMOUNT: 4 balls
TOTAL YARDAGE: 524 yards
GAUGE: 3½ stitches = 1 inch; 14 stitches
= 4 inches
NEEDLE SIZE: US #11 (8mm) or size
needed to obtain gauge
KNITTED MEASUREMENTS: Width = 6",
Length = 50"

* Yarn is worked double throughout the
scarf—this means you should hold 2
strands of yarn together as though they
are 1. *

TOP TEN REASONS WHY SEED STITCH IS OUR FAVORITE SCARF STITCH:

1. It is easy to do.

2. It has great texture.

3. It is reversible.

4. It is not too feminine.

5. It is not too masculine.

6. It is a great way to practice your knits.

7. It is a great way to practice your purls.

8. It looks harder than it is.

9. You'll impress your friends.

10. It doesn't curl at the edges.

SEED STITCH:

K1, P1 every row.

SCARF:

With #11 needle and 2 strands of yarn, cast on 25 stitches. Work in seed stitch until piece measures 50" from cast-on edge.

FINISHING:

Bind off all stitches loosely.

just for the girls

This chapter is for girls only. We tried to think of a "for boys only" chapter, but there didn't seem to be anything that was uniquely *boy*. We decided that despite the inequity, the girls deserved a chapter of their own. Let's face it—some fashion items are just more fun for girls. We decided to do four different pieces in this chapter: a swing coat with furry edges, a poncho, an A-line dress, and a cute head scarf.

The Glamorous Life is a fun swing coat that will add a little zip to any gal's wardrobe. The fuzzy edges and A-line shaping create a distinctive look that will turn heads when your girl enters a room. It is knit on large needles in garter stitch, so it knits up in a jiffy. *How Ellen Got Her Groove Back* is a simple two-rectangle poncho. It is knit loosely to create an airy, feminine look. *The Good Guest* is an A-line striped dress that we knit in bright spring colors. The A-line shape gives the dress a bit of a flowing look and is very comfortable to wear. Finally, there is *Hippie Chic*, which is an adorable head scarf that will add some flair to any girl's outfit.

the glamorous life

YARN: GGH, Relax (120 yards / 50g ball); Crystal Palace yarns, Fizz (120 yards / 50g ball)

FIBER CONTENT: Relax: 10% alpaca / 32% wool / 32% nylon / 26%; fizz: 100% polyester

COLORS: A: Relax-32; B: Fizz-9527

AMOUNT: 6 (7, 8, 9) balls color A; 3 (4, 4, 5) balls color B

TOTAL YARDAGE: 720 (840, 960, 1,080) yards color A; 360 (480, 480, 600) yards color B

GAUGE: 2 stitches = 1 inch; 8 stitches = 4 inches

NEEDLE SIZE: US #15 (10mm) or size needed to obtain gauge; circular 32" US #15 (10mm) for neck and front band ribbing

SIZES: 4–5 (6–7, 8–9, 10+)

KNITTED MEASUREMENTS: Bottom Width = 22" (23", 24", 25"), Chest Width = 15" (16", 17", 18"), Length =25" (27", 29", 31"); Sleeve Length = 11½" (12½", 14", 15")

* Color A is worked double throughout the coat—this means you should hold 2 strands of yarn together as though they are 1. *

* Color B is worked quadruple throughout the coat—this means you should hold 4 strands of yarn together as though they are 1.

Nine-year-old Cleo had recently become quite the party girl. With all sorts of upcoming birthday parties, holiday celebrations, and various other school events, she told her mother that she really didn't have anything to wear to all these things. She said that everything she owned was "too little girlish." "I need something more grown up," she told her mother, "more glamorous!" Her mom just shrugged her shoulders. But luckily Cleo's aunt, Jordana, overheard this complaint and told Cleo that she had the perfect solution. She'd been envisioning a design for a fun coat to fit a young glamour girl. It had a cute flair at the bottom and was edged in a yarn that was funky and fabulous. So the next day at work, Jordana picked out some great yarns and began knitting this coat for Cleo. Cleo loved the coat, and at the next birthday party, all of Cleo's friends told her how glamorous she looked.

BACK:

With #15 needle and 4 strands of **color B,** cast on 44 (46, 48, 50) stitches. Work in garter stitch for 10 rows. Change to 2 strands of **color A** and work in garter stitch, while **AT THE SAME TIME** decreasing 1 stitch at each end of every 8th (8th , 10th, 10th) row 7 times until 30 (32, 34, 36) stitches remain. (See step-by-step instructions.) Continue in garter stitch with no further shaping until piece measures 18" (19½", 21", 22½") from cast-on edge, ending with a WS row. SHAPE ARMHOLES: Bind off 2 stitches at the beginning of the next 2 rows. Then decrease 1 stitch at each edge, every other row, once until 24 (26, 28, 30) stitches remain. (See step-by-step instructions.) Continue to work in garter stitch until piece measures 25" (27", 29", 31") from cast-on edge, ending with a WS row. Bind off all stitches loosely.

FRONT:
(make 2, reverse shaping)

With #15 needle and 4 strands of **color B,** cast on 22 (23, 24, 25) stitches. Work in garter stitch for 10 rows. Change to 2 strands of **color A** and work in garter stitch, while **AT THE SAME TIME** decreasing 1 stitch at outside edge of every 8th (8th, 10th, 10th) row 7 times until 15 (16, 17, 18) stitches remain. (See

step-by-step instructions.) Continue in garter stitch with no further shaping until piece measures 18" (19½", 21", 22½") from cast-on edge, ending with a WS row for the left front and a RS row for the right front. SHAPE ARM-HOLES: Bind off 2 stitches at the beginning of the next row. Then decrease 1 stitch at outside edge once until 12 (13, 14, 15) stitches remain. (See step-by-step instructions.) Continue to work in garter stitch until piece measures 20" (21½", 23", 24½") from cast-on edge, ending with a RS row for the left front and a WS row for the right front. SHAPE V-NECK: For left front when worn: **Row 1:** Knit until last 4 stitches, K2tog, K2. **Row 2:** Knit. **Row 3:** Knit. **Row 4:** Knit. Repeat rows 1– 4 2 (2, 3, 3) times more times until 9 (10, 10, 11) stitches remain. Then repeat rows 1 and 2 3 (3, 2, 2) times more until 6 (7, 8, 9) stitches remain. (See step-by-step instructions.) Continue to work on remaining stitches until piece measures 25" (27", 29", 31") from cast-on edge, ending with a WS row. Bind off all stitches loosely. For right front when worn: **Row 1:** K2, SSK, knit to end. **Row 2:** Knit. **Row 3:** Knit. **Row 4:** Knit. Repeat rows 1– 4 2 (2, 3, 3) times more until 9 (10, 10, 11) stitches remain. Then repeat rows 1 and 2 3 (3, 2, 2) times until 6 (7, 8, 9) stitches remain. (See step-by-step instructions.) Continue to work on remaining stitches until piece measures 25" (27", 29", 31") from cast-on edge, ending with a WS row. Bind off all stitches loosely.

SLEEVES:

With #15 needle and 4 strands of **color B,** cast on 16 (16, 18, 18) stitches. Work in garter stitch for 10 rows. Change to 2 strands of **color A** and work in garter stitch. **AT THE SAME TIME,** increase 1 stitch at each edge, every 10th row 4 (5, 5, 6) times until you have 24 (26, 28, 30) stitches.

Note: Increase leaving 2 edge stitches on either side of work. This means you should knit 2 stitches, increase 1 stitch, knit to the last 2 stitches, increase 1 stitch, and then knit the remaining 2 stitches. Increasing like this makes it easier to sew up your seams.

When sleeve measures 11½" (12½", 14", 15") from cast-on edge, end with a WS row. SHAPE CAP: Bind off 2 stitches at the beginning of the next 2 rows. Then decrease 1 stitch at each edge, every other row once. Work 3 rows with no shaping. Bind off 2 stitches at the beginning of the next 6 (6, 8, 8) rows until 6 (8, 6, 8) stitches remain. Bind off all stitches loosely.

FINISHING:

Sew shoulder seams together. Sew sleeves on. Sew up side and sleeve seams. With a circular 32" #15 needle, 4 strands of **color B,** and RS facing, pick up 38 (42, 44, 48) stitches up the right front to beginning of V-neck shaping, place marker (pm), pick up 9 (10, 11, 12) stitches up right neck, pm, pick up 14 (14, 14, 14) stitches across back neck, pm, pick up 9 (10 , 11, 12) down left neck to end of V-neck shaping (pm), pick up 38 (42, 44, 48) stitches down left front. You will have 108 (118, 124, 134) stitches. Knit 4 rows. Bind off all stitches loosely.

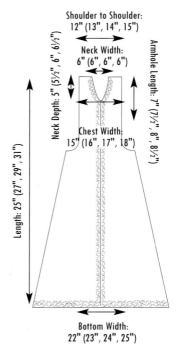

Shoulder to Shoulder: 12" (13", 14", 15")
Neck Width: 6" (6", 6", 6")
Neck Depth: 5" (5½", 6", 6½")
Armhole Length: 7" (7½", 8", 8½")
Chest Width: 15" (16", 17", 18")
Length: 25" (27", 29", 31")
Bottom Width: 22" (23", 24", 25")

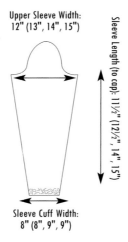

Upper Sleeve Width: 12" (13", 14", 15")
Sleeve Length (to cap): 11½" (12½", 14", 15")
Sleeve Cuff Width: 8" (8", 9", 9")

STEP-BY-STEP GUIDE TO SHAPING THE A-LINE

BACK

ROW 1 (RS): K2, SSK, knit until 4 stitches remain, K2tog, K2.
ROW 2: Knit.
ROW 3: Knit.
ROW 4: Knit.
ROW 5: Knit.
ROW 6: Knit.
ROW 7: Knit.
ROW 8: Knit.
FOR 8–9 AND 10+ SIZES ONLY:
ROW 9: Knit.
ROW 10: Knit.
FOR 4–5 AND 6–7 SIZES ONLY: Repeat rows 1– 8 6 more times.
FOR 8–9 AND 10+ SIZES: Repeat rows 1–10 6 more times.

LEFT FRONT
(left side when worn)

ROW 1 (RS): K2, SSK, knit to end of row.
ROW 2: Knit.
ROW 3: Knit.
ROW 4: Knit.
ROW 5: Knit.
ROW 6: Knit.
ROW 7: Knit.
ROW 8: Knit.
FOR 8–9 AND 10+ SIZES ONLY:
ROW 9: Knit
ROW 10: Knit.
FOR 4–5 AND 6–7 SIZES ONLY: Repeat rows 1– 8 6 more times.
FOR 8–9 AND 10+ SIZES ONLY: Repeat rows 1–10 6 more times.

RIGHT FRONT
(right side when worn)

ROW 1 (RS): Knit until 4 stitches remain, K2tog, K2.
ROW 2: Knit.
ROW 3: Knit.
ROW 4: Knit.
ROW 5: Knit.
ROW 6: Knit.
ROW 7: Knit.
ROW 8: Knit.
FOR 8–9 AND 10+ SIZES ONLY:
ROW 9: Knit.
ROW 10: Knit.
FOR 4–5 AND 6–7 SIZES ONLY: Repeat rows 1– 8 6 more times.
FOR 8–9 AND 10+ SIZES ONLY: Repeat rows 1–10 6 more times.

STEP-BY-STEP GUIDE TO SHAPING THE ARMHOLES

BACK

ROW 1 (RS): Bind off 2 stitches. Knit to end of row.
ROW 2: Bind off 2 stitches. Knit to end of row.
ROW 3: K2, SSK, knit to last 4 stitches, K2tog, K2.
ROW 4: Knit.

LEFT FRONT
(left side when worn)

You will be binding off on a RS row.
ROW 1 (RS): Bind off 2 stitches. Knit to end of row.
ROW 2: Knit.
ROW 3: K2, SSK, knit to end of row.
ROW 4: Knit.
Repeat rows 3 and 4 1 (2, 2) more times.

RIGHT FRONT
(right side when worn)

You will be binding off on a WS row.
ROW 1 (WS): Bind off 3 stitches. Knit to end of row.
ROW 2: Knit to last 4 stitches, K2tog, K2.
ROW 3: Knit.

STEP-BY-STEP GUIDE TO SHAPING THE V-NECK

LEFT FRONT
(left side when worn)

ROW 1 (RS): Knit to last 4 stitches, K2tog, K2.
ROW 2: Knit
ROW 3: Knit.
ROW 4: Knit.
Repeat rows 1– 4 2 (2, 3, 3) more times.
Then repeat rows 1 and 2 3 (3, 2, 2) more times.

RIGHT FRONT
(right side when worn)

ROW 1 (RS): K2, SSK, knit to end of row.
ROW 2: Knit.
ROW 3: Knit
ROW 4: Knit.
Repeat rows 1– 4 2 (2, 3, 3) more times.
Then repeat rows 1 and 2 3 (3, 2, 2) more times.

* When you are done with the decrease instructions, compare the length of the front piece to the length of the back. If the front and back measure the same, bind off the remaining stitches loosely. If the front is too short, continue knitting and purling until the pieces are of equal length, then bind off all stitches loosely.

how ellen got her groove back

YARN: Alchemy, Promise (440 yards / 100g ball); Trendsetter, Binario (82 yards/ 25g ball)
FIBER CONTENT: Promise: 86% kid mohair / 14% nylon; binario: 100% polyamide
COLORS: A: Promise-fuschia, B: Binario-105
AMOUNT: 1 (1, 2, 2) balls color A; 1 (1, 1, 1) ball color B
TOTAL YARDAGE: 440 (440, 880, 880) yards color A; 82 (82, 82, 82) yards color B
GAUGE: 3 stitches = 1 inch; 12 stitches = 4 inches
NEEDLE SIZE: US #13 (9mm) for body or size needed to obtain gauge; medium size crochet hook for fringe
SIZES: 4–5 (6–7, 8–9, 10+)
MEASUREMENTS: Width = 15" (16", 17", 18"), Length = 24" (25", 26", 28")

PONCHO:
(makes 2 pieces)

With #13 needle and **color A,** cast on 46 (48, 52, 54) stitches. Work in St st until piece measures 24" (25", 26", 28") from cast-on edge, ending with a WS row. Bind off all stitches loosely.

FINISHING:

Sew together as shown in the diagram. With **color B,** cut strands of yarn approximately 16" long. Put 4 strands together to make each fringe. Using a crochet hook, attach fringe evenly along the bottom of the poncho.

While going through her mother's closet, Ellen's six-year-old niece, Molly, unearthed a poncho that Ellen had made nearly twenty years ago. "I want a poncho too!" declared Molly the next time she saw Ellen. Ellen came to our store and told us that she had to make her niece a poncho but she hadn't knit in ages. In fact, she thought that the poncho Molly found might have been her last project. We told her not to worry. "Ponchos are easy, and you can knit it on big needles so it will work up in a jiffy." Ellen chose beautiful mohair in a hot color. She took a deep breath and decided to dive back into the world of knitting. Days later she returned triumphant. "I did it," she said. "I started the other night, got into a great groove, and just couldn't stop." She looked around the store and happily asked, "So what's my next project?"

Sew points A to B, C to D, E to F, and G to H.

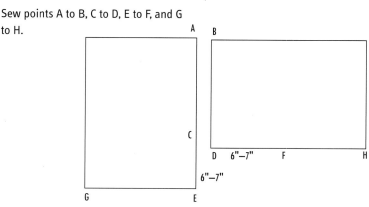

the good guest

YARN: On Line, Clip (175 yards / 100g ball)
FIBER CONTENT: 100% cotton
COLORS: A-195, B-4, C-166
AMOUNT: 2 (2, 3, 3) balls color A; 1 (2, 2, 3) ball(s) color B; 1 (2, 2, 3) ball(s) color C
TOTAL YARDAGE: 350 (350, 525, 525) yards color A; 175 (350, 350, 525) yards color B; 175 (350, 350, 525) yards color C
GAUGE: 5 stitches = 1 inch; 20 stitches = 4 inches
NEEDLE SIZE: US #6 (4mm) for body or size needed to obtain gauge; circular 16" US #6 (4mm) for neck edging
SIZES: 4–5 (6–7, 8–9, 10+)
KNITTED MEASUREMENTS: Bottom Width = 20" (21$\frac{1}{2}$", 23", 24"), Chest Width = 13$\frac{1}{2}$" (14", 14$\frac{1}{2}$", 15"), Length = 23" (25", 27", 29")

Lori's friend Laura lives in Barbados with her husband and two young daughters. Lori has an open invitation to visit Laura anytime she needs a break from the brutal New York winters, and Lori takes advantage of this almost every February when she just can't take the cold anymore. As a good guest, Lori wants to bring gifts for her host, but it isn't easy carting most gifts on an airplane. So Lori has made it a custom to bring knitted items for the girls when she visits. (A spring yarn is a must since they live in a hot climate.) For one particular visit, Lori thought matching dresses would be a cute idea, so we designed an A-line dress for them. They looked so adorable that we knew we would have to include the pattern in this book.

STRIPED ST ST:

2 rows **color B**

4 rows **color C**

2 rows **color B**

4 rows **color A**

Note: Decreases should be worked as follows: k2, ssk, knit until 4 stitches remain, k2tog, k2.

BACK AND FRONT:
(make 2)

With #6 needle and **color A**, cast on 100 (106, 114, 120) stitches. Work in garter stitch for 10 rows. Change to **color B** and begin working in striped St st pattern, while **AT THE SAME TIME** decreasing 1 stitch at each end of every 6th row 16 (18, 21, 23) times until 68 (70, 72, 74) stitches remain. (See step-by-step instructions.) Continue in striped St st with no further shaping until piece measures 16" (18", 19$\frac{1}{2}$", 21$\frac{1}{2}$") from cast-on edge, end with a WS row. SHAPE ARMHOLES: Bind off 3 stitches at the beginning of the next 2 rows. Bind off 2 stitches at the beginning of the following 2 rows. Then decrease 1 stitch at each edge, every other row, 5 times until 48 (50, 52, 54) stitches remain. (See step-by-step instructions.) Continue to work in striped St st until piece measures 20$\frac{1}{2}$" (22$\frac{1}{2}$", 24$\frac{1}{2}$", 26$\frac{1}{2}$") from cast-on edge, ending with a WS row. SHAPE NECK: Bind off the center 10 stitches. Working each side of neck separately, at the beginning of each neck edge, every other row, bind off 4 stitches once, 3 stitches once, 2 stitches once, 1 stitch once. (See step-by-step instructions.) Continue to work in striped St st on remaining 9 (10, 11, 12) stitches until piece measures 23" (25", 27", 29") from cast-on edge, ending with a WS row. Bind off all stitches loosely.

FINISHING:

Sew shoulder seams together. With #6 needle and **color A,** pick up 74 (74, 78, 78) stitches around armholes. Work 3 rows in garter stitch. Bind off all stitches loosely. Sew up side seams. With circular 16" #6 needle and **color A,** pick up 90 stitches around the neck. Work 3 rounds in garter stitch (knit 1 row, purl 1 row in the round), then bind off all stitches loosely.

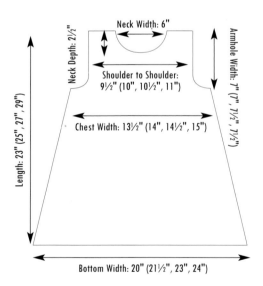

STEP-BY-STEP GUIDE TO SHAPING THE A-LINE

ROW 1 (RS): K2, SSK, knit until 4 stitches remain, K2tog, K2.

ROW 2: Purl.

ROW 3: Knit.

ROW 4: Purl.

ROW 5: Knit.

ROW 6: Purl.

Repeat rows 1– 6 15 (17, 20, 21) times more.

STEP-BY-STEP GUIDE TO SHAPING THE ARMHOLES

ROW 1 (RS): Bind off 3 stitches. Knit to end of row.

ROW 2: Bind off 3 stitches. Purl to end of row.

ROW 3: Bind off 2 stitches. Knit to end of row.

ROW 4: Bind off 2 stitches. Purl to end of row.

ROW 5: K2, SSK, knit to last 4 stitches, K2tog, K2.

ROW 6: Purl.

Repeat rows 5 and 6 4 more times.

STEP-BY-STEP GUIDE TO SHAPING THE NECK:

Remember that after binding off the center stitches, you will work one side at a time.

ROW 1 (RS): Pattern 21 (22, 23, 24) stitches. With the 20th (21st, 22nd, 23rd) stitch begin to bind off the center 10 stitches. For example, for the 4–5 size, this means you should pull the 20th stitch over the 21st stitch, and this is your first bind-off. When you are done binding off the center 10 stitches, check to make sure you have 19 (20, 21, 22) stitches on each side of the hole, including the stitch on the right-hand needle. Knit to end of row. Turn work.

ROW 2: Purl.

ROW 3: Bind off 4 stitches. Knit to end of row.

ROW 4: Purl.

ROW 5: Bind off 3 stitches. Knit to end of row.

ROW 6: Purl.

ROW 7: Bind off 2 stitches. Knit to end of row.

ROW 8: Purl.

ROW 9: Bind off 1 stitch. Knit to end of row.

ROW 10: Purl.

* When you are done with the bind-off instructions, compare the length of the front piece to the length of the back. If the front and back measure the same, bind off the remaining stitches loosely. If the front is too short, continue knitting and purling until the pieces are of equal length, then bind off all stitches loosely.

* For the other side of the neck edge, attach yarn to the remaining stitches at the center of the work (not at the side edge) and begin binding off stitches immediately. You will now be binding off with a WS row facing you. Finish neck shaping as on other side, but purling to the end of the row and knitting the even numbered rows. Bind off remaining stitches loosely.

hippie chic

YARN: Blue Sky Alpacas, Blue Sky Cotton (150 yards / 100g ball)
FIBER CONTENT: 100% cotton
COLOR: 601
AMOUNT: 1
TOTAL YARDAGE: 150 yards
GAUGE: 3 stitches = 1 inch; 12 stitches = 4 inches
NEEDLE SIZE: US #11 (8mm) for body or size needed to obtain gauge
SIZES: 4–5 (6–7, 8–9, 10+)

Sela is five years old and she has quite a few older cousins who are "into fashion." Whenever the cousins get together, they love to dress Sela up and offer wardrobe advice. At their last meeting they dressed Sela up in a flowy skirt and put a fun scarf on her head. They told her that she looked like a hippie, which was a very chic look these days. Sela nodded happily, not really knowing what they were talking about. But when she got home she adamantly told her mom, Susan, that she wanted a hippie thing to put on her head. So, Susan came to the store and we gave her this pattern to knit for Sela. Now Sela is hippie chic almost every day.

With #11 needle, cast on 81 (83, 85, 87) stitches. Knit 1 row. Bind off 20 stitches at the beginning of the next row. Knit 41 (43, 45, 49) stitches. Place last 20 stitches on a holder.

Work all rows as follows: K2, k2tog, knit until the end of the row. When 4 stitches remain, K1, K2tog, K1, K3tog.

Pull yarn through remaining loop. Place the 20 stitches on the holder back onto the needle. Reattach yarn and bind off all stitches.

blankets and pillows

Home accessories for your four- to ten-year-old? Why not? What kid doesn't like to curl up on the couch with a soft blanket and watch a movie or some television? And if they have a pillow of their very own—even better! We have included two blankets and two pillows in this chapter. *It's Easy as ABC* is a great blanket knit in garter stitch. It is knit on nice big needles so it won't take too long to complete. The center of the blanket is striped with two colors and the borders are knit in a third color. We chose a soft, spongy yarn that any kid would want to cuddle up with—no itch factor here. *Ski Bumming* is knit so there are four quadrants to this blanket. There is a knit and a purl quadrant on the bottom, and then one of each on the top. While it looks much more complicated than a stockinette and reverse

stockinette stitch pattern, even the most novice knitter should be able to master it. *Assigned Seats* is a simple pillow knit in stockinette stitch with stripes. It's just a square. You can back the pillow with some great fabric, or knit up another square either in a single color or patterned like the front. *The Care Package* is a cool colorblock pillow. It involves the intarsia technique in its simplest form—it uses only two colors at a time and the color changes are worked in a straight vertical line. When you are done working the two colors on the bottom, just cut them off and work the next two colors in the same way. We knit the back using one of the quadrant colors, but you can choose a completely different color or reuse the pattern for the front. It'll look great no matter how you back it.

it's easy as abc

YARN: GGH, Esprit (88 yards / 50g ball)
FIBER CONTENT: 100% polyamid
COLORS:
GIRL VERSION: A-20, B-14, C-22
BOY VERSION: A-13, B-8, C-7
AMOUNT: 6 balls color A; 8 balls color
B; 8 balls color C
TOTAL YARDAGE: 528 yards color A; 704
yards color B; 704 yards color C
GAUGE: 2 stitches = 1 inch; 8 stitches =
4 inches
NEEDLE SIZE: US #15 (10mm) or size
needed to obtain gauge
KNITTED MEASUREMENTS: Width =
40"; Length = 60"

* Yarn is worked double throughout the
blanket—this means you should hold 2
strands of yarn together as though they
are 1.*

Lacie, who just started school this fall, had recently, and reluctantly, agreed to part with her security blankie. As an incentive for Lacie to give up her beloved blankie, her mother, Karen, promised that she would knit her a big girl blanket. Karen and Lacie came into the store one day to pick out yarn for this project. Since this was going to be a pretty big project, Karen warned us to steer her daughter away from anything that wasn't on big needles or that might be too difficult. We showed Lacie this blanket and she fell in love with it immediately. We explained to Karen that it was knit on #15 needles, in garter stitch, and used three colors: A, B, and C. Lacie overheard us and said to Karen, "C'mon Mom, you can do it … it's easy as ABC."

GARTER STITCH STRIPE PATTERN:

4 rows knit in **color B**

4 rows knit in **color C**

BLANKET:

With #15 needle and 2 strands of **color A,** cast on 74 stitches. Work in garter stitch for 10 rows. Change to 2 strands of **color B** and work in garter stitch stripe pattern until piece measures 58" from cast-on edge. Change to 2 strands of **color A** and work 10 rows in garter. Bind off all stitches loosely.

FINISHING:

With #15 needle, 2 strands of **color A,** and RS facing, pick up 132 stitches up side edge for border. Knit for 10 rows, then bind off all stitches loosely. Repeat border along opposite edge.

ski bumming

YARN: Debbie Bliss, Cashmerino
Superchunky (80 yards / 100g ball)
FIBER CONTENT: 55% merino wool /
33% microfibre / 12% cashmere
COLORS:
GIRL VERSION: A-16003, B-16002
BOY VERSION: A-16017, B-16018
AMOUNT: 14 balls color A; 2 balls color
B
TOTAL YARDAGE: 1,120 yards color A;
160 yards color B
GAUGE: 3 stitches = 1 inch; 12 stitches =
4 inches
NEEDLE SIZE: Circular 32" US #13
(9mm) or size needed to obtain gauge;
L/11 (8mm) crochet hook
KNITTED MEASUREMENTS: Width =
40", Length = 60" (not including
edging)

Susan went skiing with her nephew, Adam, along with his friends and family, to celebrate his ninth birthday. After the third run, Susan fell and broke her leg. Well, the party for Adam was basically over, and although he knew he shouldn't feel cheated out of being the center of attention, he couldn't help it. Susan felt horrible for ruining Adam's day, so she decided to knit him something. She called us, told us she was bedridden for a while, and asked us for suggestions. We gave her the perfect blanket for him, made in soft, chunky wool. Adam loved it and forgave Susan for stealing the show. Now, he cuddles up with it while watching the ski races on TV.

BLANKET:

With #13 needle and **color A,** cast on 120 stitches. Work as follows for the next 30": **All Rows:** K60, P60 stitches. Then work as follows for the next 30": **All Rows:** P60, K60. When piece measures 60" from cast-on edge, bind off all stitches loosely.

FINISHING:

With an L crochet hook and **color B,** work 3 rows single crochet and 1 row of shrimp stitch around the edges of the blanket. Weave in all loose ends.

assigned seats

YARN: Filatura di Crosa, Zara (136 yards / 50g ball)
FIBER CONTENT: 100% merino wool
COLORS:
GIRL VERSION: A-1523, B-1461, C-1451
BOY VERSION: A-1524, B-1503, C-1472
AMOUNT: 3 balls color A; 2 balls color B; 7 balls color C
TOTAL YARDAGE: 408 yards color A; 272 yards color B; 952 yards color C
GAUGE: 4$\frac{1}{2}$ stitches = 1 inch; 18 stitches = 4 inches
NEEDLE SIZE: US #9 (5.5mm) or size needed to obtain gauge
KNITTED MEASUREMENTS: Width = 20", Length = 20"

* Yarn is worked double throughout the pillow—this means you should hold 2 strands of yarn together as though they are 1. *

Wendy's apartment is the one where all her daughters' friends come to hang out, and on Friday nights they rent movies. You can only imagine how crowded a Manhattan living room is with eight teenagers sprawled all over the couch, the two chairs, and the floor. Wendy always felt bad for the late arrivals relegated to sitting on the floor, so she decided to knit them some cushions. They were a hit, and after a few weeks, the kids settled into their preferred seats.

PILLOW:

FRONT: With #9 needle and 2 strands of **color A,** cast on 92 stitches. Work in St st stripe pattern as follows:

4 inches **color A**

4 inches **color B**

4 inches **color C**

4 inches **color B**

4 inches **color A**

Bind off all stitches loosely.

BACK: With #9 needle and 2 strands of **color C,** cast on 92 stitches and work in St st until piece measures 20" from cast-on edge. Bind off all stitches loosely.

FINISHING:

Weave ends in. Buy a pillow form that is 20" x 20". Sew 3 sides of the pillow together, place the pillow form inside and sew up the remaining side.

the care package

YARN: Crystal Palace Yarns, Cotton Chenille (98 yards / 50g ball)
FIBER CONTENT: 100% cotton
COLORS:
GIRL VERSION: A-1317, B-8211, C-2230, D-1240
BOY VERSION: A-5137, B-4021, C-8133, D-3433
AMOUNT: 1 ball color A; 4 balls color B; 1 ball color C; 1 ball color D
TOTAL YARDAGE: 98 yards color A; 392 yards color B; 98 yards color C; 98 yards color D
GAUGE: 3 1/4 stitches = 1 inch; 13 stitches = 4 inches
NEEDLE SIZE: US #10 (6mm) or size needed to obtain gauge
KNITTED MEASUREMENTS: Width = 16"; Length = 16"

* Yarn is worked double throughout the pillow—this means you should hold 2 strands of A or B together as though they are 1. *

Karen's daughter, Katie, was attending sleep-away camp for the first time. Karen, remembering how much she loved going to camp every summer, knew Katie was going to have the time of her life. A typical preteen, Katie was very concerned about how to accessorize her bed and her area in her bunk. She "needed" the perfect sleeping bag and a fun-colored trunk. Karen wanted to give Katie an early care package, so she decided to knit Katie a pillow that coordinated with her camp stuff. She chose to knit in double cotton chenille in this simple four-quadrant intarsia pattern with colors to match Katie's sleeping bag. Katie wrote home to report that her bunkmates were jealous and wanted pillows of their own.

PILLOW:

FRONT: With #10 needle and 2 strands of yarn, cast on 54 stitches as follows: 27 in **color A** and 27 in **color B.** Work in St st as follows:

Row 1 (RS): K27 B, K27 A.

Row 2: P27 A, P27 B.

When piece measures 8" from cast-on edge, end with a WS row. Change to 2 strands of **color C** and **color D** and work in St st as follows:

Row 1 (RS): K27 D, K27 C

Row 2: P27 C, P27 D.

When piece measures 16" from cast-on edge, end with a WS row, then bind off all stitches loosely.

BACK: With #10 needle and 2 strands of **color B,** cast on 54 stitches. Work in St st until piece measures 16" from cast-on edge, ending with a WS row. Bind off all stitches loosely.

FINISHING:

Weave ends in. Buy a pillow form that is 16" x16". Sew 3 sides of the pillow together, place the pillow form inside, and sew up the remaining side.

RESOURCES

Yarns used in this book can be ordered directly through the Yarn Company. However, yarns change seasonally and it is possible that some of the yarns may not be available when you're ready to place an order. Be flexible; you don't have to use the exact yarns used in a given pattern in order to get great results. Just choose a yarn or combination of yarns that achieve the required gauge. You can also contact the manufacturer for local dealers; many have helpful websites with this type of information.

The following is a list of all the manufacturers whose yarns were used in this book.

THE YARN COMPANY
2274 Broadway
New York, NY 10024
(212) 787-7878 / (888) YARNCO1
www.theyarnco.com

ALCHEMY YARNS
P.O. Box 1080
Sebastopol, CA 95473
(707) 823-3276
www.alchemyyarns.com

DEBBIE BLISS AND ONLINE YARNS
Knitting Fever/ Euro Yarns
P.O. Box 502
Roosevelt, NY 11575
(800) 645-3457
www.knittingfever.com

BLUE SKY ALPACAS YARNS
Blue Sky Alpacas, Inc.
P.O. Box 387
St. Francis, MN 55070
(888)460-8862
www.blueskyalpacas.com

CLASSIC ELITE YARNS
Classic Elite Yarns
300 Jackson Street
Lowell, MA 01852
(978) 453-2837
www.classiceliteyarns.com

CRYSTAL PALACE YARNS
Crystal Palace
160 23rd Street
Richmond, CA 94804
(800) 666-7455
www.straw.com

FILATURA DI CROSA AND TAHKI YARNS
Tahki/Stacy Charles, Inc.
7030 80th Street, Building #36
Floor 1
Glendale, NY 11385
(800) 338-9276
www.tahkistacycharles.com

GGH YARNS
Muench Yarns, Inc.
1323 Scott Street
Petaluma, CA 94954
(800)733-9276
www.muenchyarns.com

KARABELLA YARNS
Karabella Yarns, Inc
1201 Broadway
New York, NY 10001
(212) 684-2665
www.karabellayarns.com

KOIGU YARNS
Koigu Wool Designs
563295 Glenelg/Holland Town Road
RR#1
Williamsford, Ontario NOH2V0
CANADA
(888) 765-WOOL
www.koigu.com

MANOS DEL URUGUAY YARNS
Design Source
P.O. Box 770
Medford, MA 02155
(888) 566-9970

ROWAN / JAEGER YARNS
Westminster Fibers, Inc.
4 Townsend W. Suite 8
Nashua, NH 03063
(800) 445-9276
www.knitrowan.com

TRENDSETTER YARNS
16745 Saticoy Street, #101
Van Nuys, CA 91406

ZITRON YARNS
Skacel Collection
P.O. Box 88110
Seattle, WA 98138
(425) 291-9600
www.skacelknitting.com

INDEX

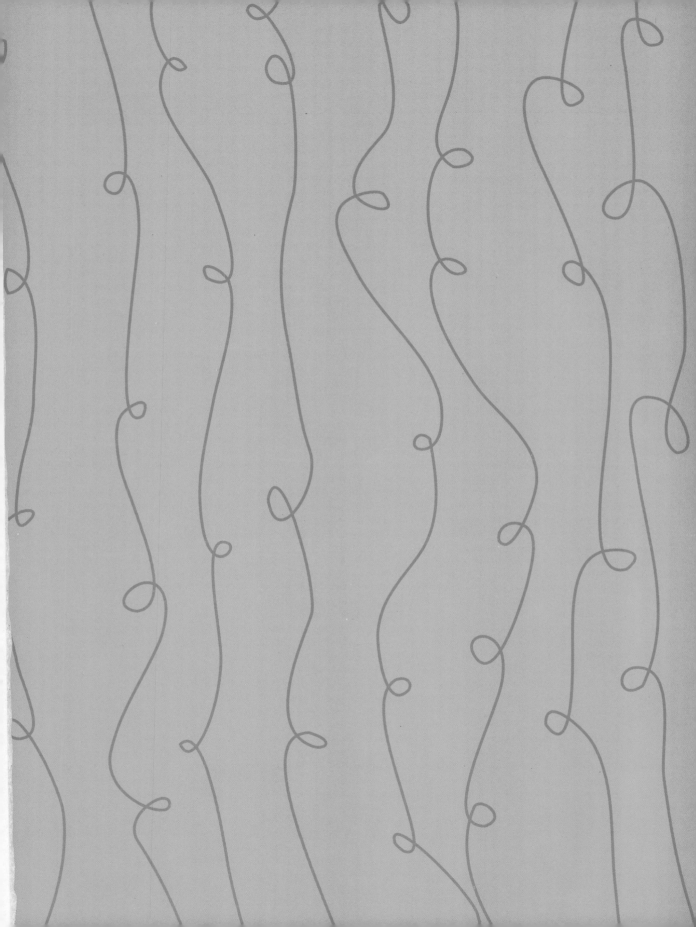

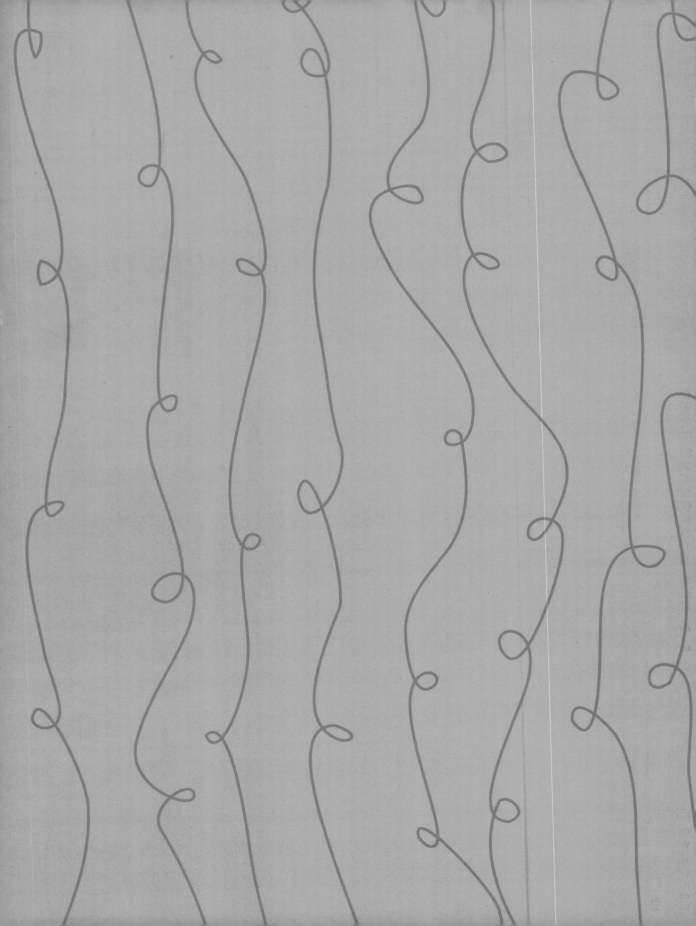